# LEADING FROM THE FRONT

Bristow Helicopters
*the first 50 years*

# LEADING FROM THE FRONT

## Bristow Helicopters
*the first 50 years*

ANDREW HEALEY

TEMPUS

Frontispiece: The Bristow Tiger – stalwart of the North Sea fleet

First published 2003

PUBLISHED IN THE UNITED KINGDOM BY:
Tempus Publishing Ltd
The Mill, Brimscombe Port
Stroud, Gloucestershire GL5 2QG
www.tempus-publishing.com

British Library Cataloguing in Publication Data.
A catalogue record for this book is available from the British Library.

ISBN 0 7524 2697 4

Typesetting and origination by Tempus Publishing.
Printed in Great Britain by Midway Colour Print, Wiltshire.

# CONTENTS

# ACKNOWLEDGEMENTS

I am indebted to Peter Pugh for permission to raid his draft of the Bristow story, which he wrote during the mid-1980s, and to Jackie Griffin, who wrote a first draft of the 'Sandstorm over the Gulf' chapter. In an effort to be objective about the 1977 pilots' strike, I depended to a large extent on the report of events from Lord McDonald's Committee of Inquiry. Sandie Richardson at Redhill was very helpful in digging out research material and photographs – even when she was under pressure in her proper job. Thanks also to 'Tugg' for permission to use his wonderful cartoons – and to Gerry Cousins, whose idea it was in the first place.

So as to maintain something approaching a narrative flow, I have left out a few of the smaller contracts in which Bristow has been involved over the past half century. For a comprehensive list of all the countries in which Bristow has operated, I recommend the website www.skyweaver.co.uk, run by Bristow avionics engineer Dave Edwards. It has also been an invaluable source of both data and illustrations for this book. Other books, such as Hugh Scanlan's *Winged Shell* and Peter Jackson's *The Sky Tramps* were useful reference sources. David Gibbings and Fred Ballam of Agusta Westland were very helpful with early photographs.

Most of all, of course, I am grateful for the contributions of many individuals (and their partners) who have given me their time, recollections and log-books – and often lunch as well. Predominant amongst those were Alan Bristow himself, Bryan Collins, George and Chris Fry, Peter Grey, Phil Hunt, Chas Newport, Mike Norris, Bill Petrie, John Odlin, Bryan Shaw, Clive Wright and Jack Woolley. Mike Norris also contributed a great deal to the editing process.

A group of long-term employees at Aberdeen, including Magnus Bentley, Tony Blanchard, Dorothy Booth, Dick Chinn, Tony Coleman, Pete Lay, John 'Tanzy' Lea, 'Baz' Leighton, Carol McBurns, Muriel Munro, Frank Sangster, Ray Smart, Audrey Smith, Dave Smith, Helen Snell, Sandra Stephenson, John Whale, Derek Whatling and John Wilson were generous with their time during my visit. Finally the Sumburgh SAR unit, including my friend Norman Leask, reminded me what a first-rate bunch of people you always find at places like that.

Here's to the next fifty years.

*Andrew Healey*
*April 2003*

# FOREWORD

In recent years, friends have asked me to what I attribute my good fortune in the helicopter business. My reply to this conversational type of question was always light-hearted and dismissive. Now, with the publication of this book covering the main events over the first fifty years in the history of Bristow Helicopters, I would like to pay tribute to those who were pivotal to both my good fortune and the success of BHL. In truth, to do justice to the question, it would take a whole book entitled 'I met a man'.

I met Ted Wheeldon for the first time in the summer of 1945, at the Royal Naval Helicopter Unit in Portland Dockyard. Eighteen months later, he was instrumental in my appointment as Westland's first helicopter test pilot. In 1952, ignoring the fact that I had been sacked by the company a few years earlier, he loaned me the use of Westland's helicopters whenever I needed to renew my pilot qualifications. Later that same year, he made me exclusive agent for the sale of the company's helicopters to the international whaling industry. The commission earned on such transactions undoubtedly enabled Air Whaling to remain solvent, through times when it would otherwise have been impossible to pay the wages. In effect, Ted Wheeldon saved my business.

Next came Group Captain Douglas Bader, DSO DFC, the managing director of Shell Aircraft, who came to my rescue when the whaling business ended so unexpectedly. It was Bader's confidence in me, at a time when the outlook was bleakest, that launched our small team of engineers and pilots onto the international offshore exploration market. Without the break that Bader gave me in 1955, to manage Shell's two WS55s in Doha, it is most unlikely that the Bristow Helicopter Group would have achieved any of the success it has since enjoyed. I have always thought of Douglas with everlasting admiration and gratitude as 'le grand patron' of the company.

Finally, and of equal ranking in importance with these gentlemen, I pay tribute to the high calibre and steadfast loyalty of all the people who worked with me during my thirty-odd-year association with Bristow Helicopters. Without them, none of the opportunities that were seized upon could ever have been successfully exploited.

*Alan Bristow*
*March 2003*

# INTRODUCTION

When I accepted the job of chief executive at Bristow, I knew I was taking up the reins of an extraordinary company. I knew it employed a group of extremely professional men and women who, over years of successfully taking on challenging worldwide contracts, had earned an enviable reputation for safe flying and engineering excellence. What I didn't fully realise was just how influential the company had become and how high its reputation stood, both within the helicopter industry and among the organisations and businesses it had supported.

When Alan Bristow formed Air Whaling in 1953, he stipulated that his business would not take short cuts. He demanded that his people would fly and maintain his helicopters 'by the book', and would never cut corners to gain a commercial edge. Before long the company became known for its professional approach and that laid the foundation for the company's successful growth. This was particularly the case in the new North Sea market in the mid-1960s.

Since then, the company has not just stuck to the rules, it has helped to create them and there are many examples where employees have made a major contribution to the safe and effective operation of helicopters the world over. For example, Bristow Helicopters 'wrote the book' on civil SAR operations and on providing cost-effective training for military helicopter pilots. Continuous improvement is a fundamental culture within the company and we continue to innovate and drive flight safety forward in ways that, in the early days, would not have been conceivable. Our Queen's Award for Enterprise this year is a fitting tribute to everyone's continuing professionalism and commitment.

Alan Bristow also said that, to make a decent return on investment, his company would have to operate around the globe. That has certainly proved to be the case and there cannot be many regions of the world over which, at one time or another, a Bristow helicopter has not hovered. Where we have handed operations over to local people, they have inherited our values and built new businesses using the Bristow model.

Flying helicopters, especially in such demanding environments, is never a risk-free exercise. Inevitably, we have suffered our share of tragedies and it would be remiss of me, if I did not pay tribute to the Bristow people, their families and friends who have been affected. It is to them, as well as to all present and former employees and their families, that I dedicate this book.

*Keith Chanter*
*Chief Executive*
*Bristow Helicopters*
*June 2003*

'That bloody stores computer's on the blink again . . . ' (Copyright: Tugg, 1982-2003)

The Sikorsky YR4B – Alan Bristow's first type-rating. (Photo Fleet Air Arm Museum)

## CHAPTER ONE

# FIRST FLIGHT

Attacks by torpedo or gunfire are occupational hazards for any merchant seaman during times of war. By the time four ships have been sunk under you in two years, however, you may be starting to think that someone has it in for you.

The first time young Alan Bristow, a deck officer cadet with the British India line, was torpedoed, his ship's bow was badly damaged. She was 400 miles off Nova Scotia and the crew's only course of action was to shore up the collision bulkhead with timber and limp, stern-first and through thick fog, towards Halifax. During the next eighteen months further ships were sunk under the young mariner – twice by torpedo and once by gunfire. By then, he was wondering how much longer his luck could last.

On the day war was declared in 1939, Alan was celebrating his sixteenth birthday. A year later, he abandoned ambitions of a place at Cambridge to join British India. Over the next three years he served in the North Atlantic, North Africa and Burma campaigns. As well as his Canadian adventure, he was faced with having to duck-dive under a burning oil slick in the Bay of Bengal and, during the North African landings, enduring relentless dive-bombing attacks.

During a welcome spot of home leave, Alan and three fellow cadets agreed that they would all be better off serving somewhere else, where they might have more of a fighting chance. They were unaware that the Merchant Navy was regarded as an all-but-combatant service at the time, and that leaving it because you didn't like being sunk was regarded as tantamount to desertion. In June 1943, therefore:

> We went to see the RAF in Russell Square, London, armed with a story about getting fed-up with studying at Cambridge and wanting to see some action. I was called in first because my name started with B and was soon told the air force was doing quite nicely for pilots, Mr Bristow, but would I like to be an air gunner? I really didn't fancy that: said, 'No thank you' and left.

One of his colleagues agreed to sign on and was later killed, while the other two returned to the Merchant Navy. Disappointed, Alan set off back to Victoria Station, en route walking through Trafalgar Square. There, on a wall in Cockspur Street, he noticed a big white banner urging Londoners to 'Join The Fleet Air Arm Pilot "Y" Scheme'. Why not become a naval aviator instead, he thought?

He walked in the nearby door and up the stairs, to find a Chief Petty Officer and a bored-looking RNVR Lieutenant Commander. He trotted out his Cambridge story and, after a medical and interview, sat down to take an aptitude test; which involved moving a stick to keep a dot in a randomly moving circle. 'You've done this before!' accused the Chief as the two remained firmly welded together.

Alan passed the interview and, in June 1943, was sent down to join pilot course No.56 at HMS *St Vincent*, a training establishment at Gosport in Hampshire.

*We were a strong contingent of 80 and, because I had already built up some sea-time, I was appointed course leader. As the training progressed, the campaign medals I was due from my service in the North Atlantic, North Africa and Burma campaigns turned up. This was noticed by our training Chief Petty Officer, a fearsome man by the name of Wilmot, who reported me to the Training Commander for wearing unauthorised medals. I told him the truth and, fortunately, he didn't make the connection that I might be AWOL from the Merchant Navy. For a while, that was the end of the matter.*

Course 56 travelled to Canada, to Saint Eugene outside Montreal, to learn to fly the Cornell Ranger monoplane. Alan won his wings in July 1944 and, alongside several others with 'above average' flying marks, was asked if he'd like to volunteer to fly helicopters. His immediate reaction, honed through his wartime experiences to date,

Alan Bristow's helicopter course at Floyd Bennett Field, New York. Left to right, standing at rear: Cliff Penfold, AEB, Harry Little. Sitting: Len Page, Lt Stewart, Eric Andrews. (Photo Fleet Air Arm Museum)

A Sikorsky YR4B practises deck-landings to HMS *Vanguard*. (Photo Fleet Air Arm Museum)

was to say 'no'. The Commander (Flying) was livid and threw him out of his office, along with three other rebels – Cliff Penfold, Harry Little and Eric Andrews. The next day he brought them back in and ordered them to go anyway. 'We were sent to New York to learn to fly the Sikorsky YR4B helicopter. Our base was the Floyd Bennett Field Coastguard base – now better known as JFK International Airport'. Although he graduated, he wasn't enamoured with the idea of rattling along at low level and 70-odd knots so, when he got back to England, he asked his father – a Commodore who had been in charge of Malta's dockyard during the earlier siege – if he could help get him transferred back to 'fixed wing'.

Paternal influence paid off and Sub Lieutenant Bristow RNVR was appointed to HMS *Trumpeter*, a fleet auxiliary carrier armed with Hellcats and Seafires, and due to sail for action in the Far East. A serious bout of hepatitis put him in isolation for six weeks, however, and he was unable to join. Once recovered, he was sent to 771 Naval Air Squadron at HMS *Tern*; an air station near Twatt in the Orkneys.

From there he was able to fly both Seafires and, when the opportunity arose, the YR4B, which became known in the UK as the Hoverfly. He carried out the first deck-landings of a helicopter on a frigate, HMS *Helmsdale*, and on a battleship at sea – the top of 'A' turret of HMS *Anson*. 'The crew swung 'B' turret out of his way but I still had less than three feet clearance.'

Shortly after VE day, Lt Neil Fuller and Sub-Lt Bristow were appointed to 'Haslemere Flight', a helicopter section of 771 Squadron, and ordered to fly the unit's two YR4Bs from Twatt down to an air station at Worthy Down, near Winchester. The flight was subsequently based at Portland Dockyard, with orders to progress deck-landing techniques and gun calibration trials.

One lump or two? A YR4B dispenses tea and buns at Worthy Down. (Photo Fleet Air Arm Museum)

On the slipway at Portland. (Photo Fleet Air Arm Museum)

Among the young pilots who passed through Portland was Sub-Lt Alan Green RNVR, an individual who would play an important part in the later development of Bristow Helicopters. His first order from Sub-Lt Bristow, he later recalled, was to sweep all the seaweed from the slipway. It was during this period that Bristow married Jean, a Chief Petty Officer Wren who worked in the Worthy Down clothing store.

While flying the Y4B at Portland, two directors of Westland Aircraft, one of whom was Ted Wheeldon, paid a visit from nearby Yeovil. The aeroplane manufacturer was interested in the potential of the helicopter and was conscious that wartime Seafire and Wyvern production would not last much longer. Wheeldon hinted that, at some point in the future, there might be an opportunity for Alan to work for them.

The young pilot had just been offered a permanent naval commission, but his father advised him that a non-Dartmouth background would not help him progress in the fierce competition for higher rank. In that case he decided to apply for 'demob' and left the Navy, as a Lieutenant RNVR, in February 1946.

After a short period spent working for RK Dundas in London, where he sold all manner of aviation equipment on a basic salary plus commission, Alan saw an advertisement in *Flight International* for the Westland test pilot job. He applied straightaway and, after a gruelling interview process alongside at least twenty fellow applicants, was asked what salary he expected. He swiftly offered to work for £50 less than whatever the going rate was. He got the job – on £750 a year.

Westland's chief test pilot at the time was Harald Penrose – 'a wonderful man', recalls Alan – who noted the aviator's arrival at Yeovil. 'A brashly confident, 23 year-old Lieutenant tore into the works in a tatty little car, and made it clear he believed he had more and better helicopter experience than anyone else Westland was likely to get. Certainly his enthusiasm was obvious.'

Alan was soon sent to Bridgeport, Connecticut, to find out about test-flying in Sikorsky's latest S51 helicopter, which Westland had agreed to build under licence. In February 1947 he returned and, by April, the machine had followed him back to Yeovil.

Taken at a helicopter open day at Westland's Yeovil plant. Alan Bristow is in the Dragonfly with Jean in front. Peter Garner is eighth from left, Harald Penrose is tenth and Len Swain is seated on the right. (Photo Thompson Bennett)

Penrose remembers his first flight in the helicopter:

*On 18 April G-AJHW was ready for its first flight and I joined Alan as a passenger. During the preceding days he had supervised much of the final assembly work and patiently explained to me the technology and piloting techniques. We took off and, at first, just hovered. Then we shut down and checked all the mechanisms, to make sure nothing had worked loose. After a bit more hovering we tried a gentle circuit.*

*Much performance testing followed. Presently both Pete Garner and I also learned how to handle it – with no great difficulty, as it turned out, for the technique was similar to demonstrating a Lysander's slow descent. Indeed our early problem was trying to prevent the helicopter going backwards. However, the pressure to maintain our own test flying programme was so strong at the time, that we had little time for helicoptering, so Bristow became very much a lone hand. Soon he was made Chief Pilot (Helicopters), reporting to me.*

Anticipating military demand, Westland began serial production of thirty WS51s (adding the 'W' for Westland), and allocating the type name 'Dragonfly'. In January 1949 the Royal Navy ordered thirteen of them for 705 Squadron, based at Culdrose Naval Air Station in Cornwall, and the RAF took another three.

During these early days Westland, imbued with an adventurous spirit through its dynamic Chairman, Sir Eric Mensforth CBE, was keen to demonstrate the helicopter's versatility to anyone who would pay attention. Penrose again:

HW – Westland's first S51. (Photo Agusta Westland)

On finals to Yeovil.

*During the summer of 1947 we arranged a big demonstration at Harrods' sports ground at Barnes, on the banks of the Thames in West London. Until then few people had even seen a helicopter fly, let alone thought about its potential. Government ministers, ministry officials, Members of Parliament, heads of research establishments, airline operators, senior military officers and dozens of reporters were invited, and royally entertained in a huge marquee.*

*In bright sunshine, they watched a flying programme that Alan had devised to show off every aspect of the WS51s versatility. A crewman climbed a rope ladder into the hovering machine and another was winched up, then down into a dinghy on the river. Then a netted load, slung underneath the helicopter, was placed inside a marked circle. For the benefit of Trinity House – the agency responsible for lighthouses – it hovered alongside a buoy while a crewman replaced the lamps. For the Red Cross and Army it flew with external stretcher pods fitted above the skids. Meanwhile I struggled through a running commentary. Afterwards Pete Garner joined Alan and, together, they gave familiarity flights to scores of delighted visitors.*

Most of the young pilot's time was now spent trying to convince potential customers of the value of the helicopter. Demonstrations were given to the armed services, the police, the Royal National Lifeboat Institution and British European Airways. BEA, destined to become the first UK commercial operator, was at the time already

Alan Bristow meets George Russell Fry. (Photo Agusta Westland)

experimenting with a Bell 47. Alan became the first pilot to land on the roof of the BBC at Portland Place, in Regent's Park and Horseguards Parade – 'bags of room of course, but impressive for the punters' – and to fly down the Thames during the Henley Regatta, on charter to British Movietone News.

He won a great deal of media coverage after landing on the roof of the Olympia Exhibition Centre in London. There he was approached by a young accountant – George Russell Fry – a decorated former RAF Lancaster pilot who was fascinated with the whole business of rotary-wing aviation. A preoccupied Bristow suggested they meet up, once the fuss surrounding the helicopter's arrival had died down.

Alan attracted more publicity when he delivered supplies to three lighthouse keepers, who had been isolated for nearly a month by atrocious weather on Wolf Rock, eight miles off Lands End. For forty-eight hours the weather – and the orders of the Commanding Officer of Culdrose Naval Air Station – prevented Bristow from taking off. In the end, frustration got the better of him and he lifted off anyway, at 0600 on 7 February 1948, into the teeth of a 60 knot gale. With an eye to publicity for the helicopter he also told the *Daily Express*, which sent a photographer to take pictures from a Rapide.

Alan reached the lighthouse and his mechanic Les Swain – Westland's chief service engineer and a regular crewman on many of these early flights – began to lower the supplies to the narrow lantern gallery by winch. The first two loads were successfully delivered but, while removing the third, one of the keepers forgot the brief and fastened the cable hook to the gallery's rail. The immediate and dramatic result was that the helicopter became practically uncontrollable. As it veered helplessly towards the lighthouse in 60mph gusts, at one point bouncing a wheel off the lantern cover, Alan yelled to Swain to lean out of the door and cut the wire with his cutters. The WS51 popped clear 'like a champagne cork' and the pair returned to Culdrose to face the music.

Bristow was reprimanded by the CO, Capt. Black, for disobeying orders and awarded the Royal Aero Club's silver medal for valour. Penrose thought it should have been a gold one.

Alan and Jean's daughter Lynda was born in May 1948, while Bristow was in Brussels on Westland business. Penrose was hurriedly recruited to take Jean to hospital – and was misidentified as the father by the midwife. This became a standing joke between the two families for many years.

A September 1948 publicity stunt involved a joint aeroplane and helicopter race from St Paul's Cathedral, in central London, to the Place des Invalides in the centre of Paris. At that time regular airline flights from Northolt to Orly took an hour, but it could take a further two or three hours to clear customs and travel to and from the city centres – a schedule not too much at odds with that of today. The previous fastest time, set in 1921, had been two hours taken by an amphibian aeroplane, which took off from the Thames at Westminster and landed on the Seine at the other end.

The Wolf Rock rescue. (Photo Express Newspapers)

The Westland, Bristol and Gloster aircraft companies all saw the scope for positive publicity and joined forces to set a new record. Harald Penrose remembers it well.

*After much negotiation the rival to Westland's WS51, a Bristol Sycamore, was positioned in a bomb-site car park, adjacent to St. Paul's Cathedral, ready for take-off to Biggin Hill in Kent. There a speed record-breaking Gloster Meteor awaited, its jets burning, poised to fly to Paris Orly airport. At the end of the runway waited Alan Bristow in his WS51, ready to sprint to the winning post at the Place des Invalides.*

*With a 500ft cloud base at Orly and the top of the Eiffel Tower obscured, there was a 90 minute delay in starting. At 12.30pm, however, a letter from the Lord Mayor of London, addressed to his opposite number in Paris, was handed to Sycamore pilot Eric Swiss. He then pulled a dramatic vertical take-off above the cathedral's dome.*

*The flight to Biggin Hill took nine and a half minutes. The letter was handed over and away shot the splendidly moustachioed Bill Waterton inside the Meteor. Despite overshooting Orly in the mist at his first attempt, he landed in 27 ½ minutes. After a lightning twelve-second letter transfer, a jubilant Bristow managed to cross the line in his WS51, eight and a half minutes later!*

The whole journey had taken forty-six minutes and forty-five seconds. Because the race involved two classifications of aircraft – fixed and rotary-wing – the 'record' could not be officially ratified. Nevertheless it was recognised by both the Royal

Commemorating the London to Paris race.

Aero Club and Aero Club de France and, that evening, everyone was royally wined and dined at the latter's premises in Paris. 'Oh boy!' recalls Alan, 'What a night!' Despite all the publicity, the triumph of knocking nearly two hours from what was already seen as a fairly impractical record, did not herald the immediate revolution in world air travel that some were hoping for.

Bristow continued to fly manoeuvres that, these days, just would not be allowed. In the spring of 1949 he demonstrated the WS51 at the Paris Air Show, with daily passenger flights and demonstrations. He fell foul of the authorities when he accepted a dare from the French President's daughter, jet pilot Jacqueline Auriol, to fly her through the arches of the Eiffel Tower. 'There was plenty of room', he insisted and, after proving that point, he pulled up into as near a loop as any helicopter, at that time, could manage. Aware that such flying was strictly prohibited, he mockingly held his wrists out for handcuffs as he climbed out.

In Switzerland, while demonstrating the WS51 to the Swiss Army, he landed so high on a mountain ledge that he had no surplus power with which to lift. Undeterred, he launched the aircraft down the steep slope, much like a hang-glider, so as to build the necessary take-off speed.

It was while he was at Westland that his wartime career finally came back to haunt him. At his rented chicken farm – a useful supplement to his meagre test pilot's salary – near the Somerset village of Charlton Mackrell, Alan was visited by a Naval Lieutenant and a Master-at-Arms and arrested on a charge of 'desertion in the face of the enemy'. The Royal Navy had discovered how he had left the Merchant Navy without permission. Although they personally understood the circumstances and were sympathetic, their duty was to bring him before a disciplinary hearing in London.

Desertion is a serious matter and Alan was worried. However, standing in front of the board, he explained how he had come to make the switch. 'I was fed up with being sunk', he said, 'and wanted to be able to face the enemy on more-or-less equal terms'. The five board members went into a huddle. Finally the Chairman – a Rear-Admiral who had asked him if he was Commodore Bristow's son – announced the matter was closed and would he like to join them in the Wardroom for a pink gin?

Exonerated, Alan returned to Somerset to continue test-flying WS51s, which by now were rolling off the assembly line. However his time with the company came to an abrupt end – after something of a disagreement with the company's sales manager.

Alan was organising a helicopter demonstration in Brussels and needed, as usual, to make sure he had enough engineers, firefighters, passenger handlers and refuellers for the job. He phoned the sales manager to find out how many people he would need to fly during his programme of short familiarisation flights. 'None of your business', was the retort. After explaining why it was indeed his business, the manager slammed the phone down on him.

Alan went white: this was not the first time the man had been rude to him.

*I got up, walked the quarter of a mile to his office and demanded an apology. He told me to get out so I punched him on the jaw and laid him out on the floor. I then walked down the corridor to the managing director's office and told Johnny Fearn what I'd done.*

Test-flying the WS51. (Photo Ron Francis)

Fearn stood there open-mouthed but Penrose, who was also there, was sympathetic – the manager was universally disliked. However, Alan was told he had better go home, under suspension, for a couple of weeks while things cooled down. At the end of this period Fearn called Alan and said the directors had decided, after all, that they had to let him go. He wouldn't even be allowed back onto the site to collect his belongings. Undeterred, Alan borrowed a friend's Piper Super Cub, flew it to land on Westland's runway, taxied up to his office, collected his things and flew off again.

At the grand old age of twenty-six, Alan Bristow was now unemployed. As he was to find out over the next few weeks, he was also practically unemployable. He got a job at Bristol, where they built the Sycamore, but never got to fly the machine. After two weeks he was summoned to the managing director's office, where he was told that the SBAC (Society of British Aircraft Constructors) had blackballed him as a result of his assault on the Westland man. 'But you knew about all that when you hired me!' he exclaimed. 'Yes I know', explained the director, 'but the Society is making life very difficult for me and we're going to have to let you go. We'll pay you a couple of months' salary and …' – 'Shove it up your arse!' was the angry response. Alan was furious that they had allowed themselves to be intimidated by the SBAC.

He went for an interview with Percival Aircraft, which was investigating helicopter designs, and was swiftly accepted to test-fly for them. However SBAC's influence was once more brought to bear and he lasted less than a week, never getting near the aircraft. There followed a couple of odd jobs, one of which involved tuning a Piper Super Cruiser for the King's Cup race, but he needed a proper job to support his growing family – his son Laurence was born in 1952.

He then contacted a friend, Jean Boulet, who was chief test pilot for France's Sud Aviation. Bristow had met Boulet while still in the Navy, when he had been sent to Paris to fly a German helicopter, the twin-rotored Focke–Achgelis FA-61, which was a 'spoil-of-war'. 'That was a hell of a good aircraft,' he recalls. 'Years ahead of its time, but very complicated. We scared ourselves rigid on one occasion when we heard an enormous "bang!" and thought the aircraft was about to break up. We landed immediately but couldn't find a thing wrong with it.'

Boulet couldn't care less about the SBAC. He told the Englishman that he had heard a man called Henri Boris was setting up a new business, Hélicop-Air, in Paris to market the Hiller 360 helicopter throughout Europe. Alan tracked him down, struck up an immediate rapport and was soon taken on to set up a training school.

Before long Bristow was chief pilot, chief engineer, chief salesman and – since Boris was planning to make a killing in the aerial spraying market – chief spraying expert. Although helicopters are more expensive spraying vehicles than aeroplanes, at the time they were considered more efficient – the recirculating downwash from the blades ensures that the leaves are thoroughly coated. Hélicop-Air was agent for US manufacturer Hiller and, before long, Boris and Bristow had nineteen Hiller 360s on the company strength.

As well as spraying crops in France and North Africa, Alan towed water-skiers down the Seine and trailed advertising banners. He took thousands of aerial photographs and, on one occasion, took part in a professionally choreographed 'Ballet for Helicopters', which was performed in front of large crowds at Orly. He also flew a promotional tour for wool manufacturer 'Laine de Pingouin', which involved landing in dozens of village squares in Northern France and handing out free samples of woollen socks.

Crop spraying in a Hiller.

In 1949, Alan was sent to French Indo-China to meet a prospective Hiller customer – a puppet prince by the name of Bao Dai. He flew out to meet the young playboy and soon decided that he was a hot sales prospect. However, he had nothing to demonstrate to him. Alan phoned Boris and sent a succession of telegrams, pleading for a helicopter to be sent out from Paris. Meanwhile the military was showing interest in the Hiller: in particular Médecin-Général Robert and several unit commanders expressed a strong interest in seeing one.

*Dear old Boris wouldn't bite and told me to come home. I didn't have a return ticket and he, believing I did, refused to send me another. We had a row over the phone, fell out and parted company – with me on the other side of the world. Convinced I could sell the type to the French military I got straight on the phone to Bill Vincent, vice-president of sales at the Hiller corporation, and tried to talk him into sending a 360 to me in Indo-China, on a sale-or-return basis.*

*It took a lot of arguing over a very bad phone line but he eventually agreed, and one was duly freighted out, together with a set of over-skid Stokes rescue litters. With the help of the manual and an Armée de l'Air mechanic, I got the thing assembled and rigged in a hangar and started to test-fly it from Tan Son Nhut airfield: now Ho Chi Minh International Airport. We flew a number of demonstration flights from there. Bao Dai was very excited and asked me to land in the gardens of his various palaces, so that he could show off. He never did buy one, though.*

The Army, however, was still a strong prospect. Out at the airport one day, Alan was tracking the Hiller's rotors when the CO of a French squadron ran up and pleaded for his help. Would he fly out to rescue some casualties from a French Foreign Legion parachute regiment, that had become trapped by the Viet Cong? 'It's not far,' he assured him. 'Only 60 miles.'

*I refused immediately, as I had no intention of getting involved in another war. But the Colonel was adamant. He offered me a parachute, a revolver and hand grenades – even an escort of Thunderbolt fighters to soften up the area with napalm.*

Eventually Alan gave in and mounted up. He was wearing his 'tropical rig' of white shirt, shorts and stockings, and now armed to the teeth.

*I flew out there at 3,500ft, out of the range of small-arms fire, with the Thunderbolts flashing down my sides every so often. When I found the Paras, by now under mortar fire, I spiralled in to land amongst the slit trenches, landed, and shut down. Before I could climb out, the CO ran over and asked me to take four of the worst wounded back with me – double the capacity of the Hiller. As I struggled to get them organised, more than once I had to dive for cover in a sodden trench, as mortar shells fell close by.*

*Some time later, with two casualties in the Stokes litters and one strapped either side of me in the cabin, I tried to take off. Of course I had no spare power: The helicopter was hopelessly overweight and the weather conditions, as usual, didn't help. There were trees at about 100ft on all sides. By over-revving the engine I managed to get the skids light on the ground, then skidded and bounced along the grass until I built up enough translational lift to haul the thing up into*

Alan Bristow
in combat
gear.

*the tree-tops. It was a do-or-die effort. I picked up plenty of greenery as the helicopter struggled through the branches – over-powered, over-revved, over-temped, over-everything – but it stayed airborne and I managed to keep going. On the way home I don't think I got more than 20ft above the trees, so thank God no one shot at me then.*

When Alan got back, trembling as a result of his exertions, a medical officer – Capt. Valérie André – took charge of his casualties. One of them had a bullet wound in his forehead and André asked the Englishman if he'd care to watch the operation she was about to undertake. He agreed, as the operating theatres were the only areas in the camp that were air-conditioned. However, when the doctor exposed the soldier's skull, he fainted flat-out on the floor. 'It was partly shock, partly exhaustion.'

When he had recovered, Alan flew back to the battlefield and made a total of five trips to evacuate casualties. Eventually a gunboat was sent up-river to retrieve the rest of the Paras, but the Hiller had proved its worth to General Robert and, over lunch at his residence a few days later, he ordered twelve of them. The young pilot was also given a temporary commission into the French Foreign Legion and, later, the Croix de Guerre for his evacuation exploits.

Boris and Bristow soon patched up their quarrel and Alan returned to Paris, to train the pilots to fly these new machines. In 1950 he returned to Indo-China once more to hand over his job as *de facto* squadron commander to one of his ex-students, Capt. Louis Santini. Later that year he finally returned to Jean in Somerset, with enough tax-free funds to buy a house and with a new idea. He had picked it up from a fellow-occupant of the trench he had sheltered in during one of the rescue missions – an ex-SS Paratrooper and Legionnaire by the name of Wolfgang.

## CHAPTER TWO

# DOWN SOUTH

Wolfgang was nearing the end of his tour of duty in Indo-China. Apart from making sure he survived his last few days, his thoughts were turning to what he might do after he got back to Germany.

'I'll tell you where the real money is,' he confided to his English companion. 'Whaling. After this hell, I'm off down south with my brother. Lot more peaceful there.' Sometime later in Saigon, Alan met Wolfgang again and, over a great deal of wine, Wolfgang explained that he was joining his brother in Kiel, to embark on a whaling expedition to the Antarctic for Greek shipping magnate Aristotle Onassis. He explained how the business of whaling worked, how catcher boats were dispatched ahead of the main factory ship to look for the beasts – and how difficult it often was for them to find their quarry.

*I thought about this for a long time and, when I got home, talked this potential market over with Jean. Then out of the blue came a phone call from Bill Vincent at Hiller, who also told me that Onassis was indeed considering helicopters for that role. He was clearly a strong prospect. As soon as I could, I travelled to Hamburg and met up with Hans Reuter, who was in charge of an Onassis team converting a T2 tanker into a whaling factory ship and a dozen ex-Canadian Navy corvettes into whale catchers.*

Reuter welcomed the Englishman's approach, immediately saw what he had in mind and suggested he went to Paris to meet a Mr Cokinnis. He, in turn, sent Alan to Monte Carlo to meet Onassis himself. Over dinner in a nightclub, Onassis discussed his ideas and then sent him on to New York to meet Mr Konialides, who was in charge of the shipping company. Konialides issued Alan with a Lincoln Continental and enough dollars to last him six months, and sent him off to trawl the US helicopter manufacturers for a suitable helicopter, with which to support Olympic Whaling during the forthcoming Antarctic summer.

He visited Frank Piasecki in Philadelphia, whose 'flying banana' proved to be too big. To Connecticut next, where Igor Sikorsky's S51 and S52 were relatively untried,

A whale catcher making heavy weather.

particularly in the unforgiving environment they would find in the Antarctic. Then west, to visit Bell and its B47H at Fort Worth in Texas, and finally to Hiller in Palo Alto, California.

After flying them all over a four-week period the choice, in Alan's mind, boiled down to either the Bell or the Hiller 360A. His final recommendation to buy the Hiller rested on its excellent hands–off stability, derived from the two small aerofoil sections mounted on the rotor mast at right angles to the blades. He flew back to New York to report to Konialides – who was immediately suspicious to see him back, less than halfway through his allotted six months.

Nonetheless, his report was accepted and Onassis ordered the Hiller, while Alan flew back to Germany to help Reuter design a flight deck on the stern of factory ship *Olympic Challenger*. At this late stage there was no room for a hangar so, when on deck for any length of time, the helicopter would have to be covered up. To stop the wooden blades flapping, Alan designed padded clamps which were secured, via poles, to eye bolts mounted on the flight deck.

Alan had asked Hiller for a direction finder and HF radio, with a long weighted aerial for streaming behind the fuselage, as well as an experienced airframe and engine mechanic. He also ordered a manually-operated radio location beacon, known during its wartime service with RAF Coastal Command as a 'Gibson Girl', and a 'Frankenstein' waterproof immersion suit.

Rather than sell him its prototype suit, the Frankenstein Rubber Co. offered Alan a £6,000 fee, on condition that he spent a total of thirty hours in the Antarctic waters, in amongst the pack ice, while wearing their product. He would also have to wear half of the two-piece suit all day, in order to check how its water-repellent properties were affected by daily wear-and-tear and, as they put it, 'human juices'. Commercial instincts already to the fore, and calculating that body odour aboard a whaling ship might not be considered the worst of social crimes, he quickly agreed.

Alan arrived in Montevideo, Uruguay, in November 1950 to await the Hiller (N178H) and the *Olympic Challenger*. He was put up in one of the best hotels in town and given the use of another Lincoln Continental. The Hiller soon arrived, in crates, followed soon after by the Hiller engineer. Joe Soloy, who went on to found his own turbine engine company, ruefully admitted to a minimal knowledge of helicopter assembly techniques. An ex-Marine, he had been completing a veteran's six-week training course on part of the Hiller production line at Palo Alto, when he heard about the well-paid Antarctic opportunity. In sore need of extra cash to help him pay for an expensive operation on his son's toes, he had immediately volunteered.

With so little helicopter experience, Soloy wasn't going to be much help in assembling the Hiller so, once again, Alan did all the work, while Joe read out instructions from the accompanying manual. The machine took shape, as did the HF radio assembly, and the pair flight-tested both until Alan was satisfied.

The first season, from October 1951 to May 1952, was spent aboard the *Olympic Challenger* factory ship. The vessel displaced some 100,000 tons and featured a vast open deck area, reached via a slipway and an opening in the stern known as 'Hell's Gate'. This was dedicated to the gruesome tasks of rendering the blubber and bones of the creatures and butchering the carcass. Accompanying the ship was a fleet of at least a dozen whale-catchers, former anti-submarine corvettes which weighed 1,500 tons apiece and which, with blistering acceleration, could make a top speed of about 17 knots.

On the hunt.

Hell's gate.

Flensing.

Lookouts would direct the gunner, who was invariably the boat's owner/captain as well, towards the quarry and put him in the best position possible to fire. From as close a range as possible, a breech-loading gun would shoot into the whale a 175lb harpoon with an explosive fragmenting head. It often took more than one to finish the job. Once dead, the carcasses were inflated with compressed air and 'tagged' with a flag for later pick-up by a tow-boat for delivery to the factory ship.

The Hiller immediately added an extra dimension to the hunt. From height and in often unlimited visibility, Alan could see a long way further than the catchers. He could fly search patterns out to sixty, sometimes eighty miles ahead and, from an altitude of 500ft, could spot a whale's 'blow' at up to eight miles. Other clues were provided by patches of Krill – a member of the prawn family and the whale's staple diet – in the water and the presence of several species of bird.

Although many of the ship's crew were sceptical about the worth of a helicopter on board, they soon realised its value as a spotter – not just for finding whales but to identify the best way through the pack ice. During this first season, as the fleet struggled to break through the ice into the Ross Sea, Alan was able to direct the ship's passage up to five miles ahead. The fleet of fifteen vessels made it through, in line astern, in record time.

Alan learnt his lessons the hard way in the Antarctic. He learned about flying over the vast desolate areas and the need to keep, in his head, a rough bearing from the mother ship, so he could find his way back if the weather changed – which it could do almost in an instant. He learned that landing in snow, whether on land or on an ice floe, could blow up clouds of the stuff, creating a 'white-out' which was impossible to see through.

Butchering a blue whale.

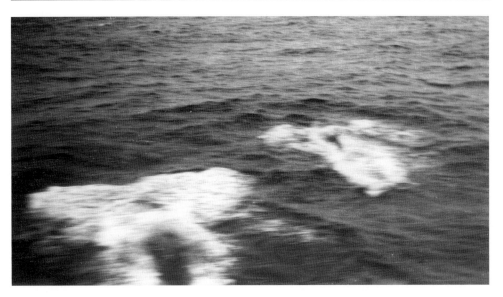

'Footprints' from a whale's tail.

He came to put great reliance in his Frankenstein suit: without it he would have little chance of surviving a ditching. Alan's suit-testing routine, of jumping into a floating rubber ring tied to the companionway, initially caused much amusement amongst the crewmembers. Undeterred, he completed the contract requirements. His feedback turned out to be of great value and the trial was deemed a success. The Frankenstein Rubber Co. changed its name to the Victoria Rubber Co. and soon won a large contract for its suits from the Royal Navy – and eventually from Bristow Helicopters.

A day's work in the Antarctic began as the summer sun rose above the horizon – at these latitudes it hardly dipped. After an 0300 briefing from the whaling manager, who would summarise the whereabouts of the fleet and identify the target area, Bristow and Soloy would inspect the helicopter on the exposed flight deck. Alan would remove the full-length blade covers and the clamps and poles, check that no ice had formed on the exposed parts and then, having learnt during wartime never to take his next meal for granted, head below for a good breakfast. At around 0500, wearing his Frankenstein suit, balaclava, sheepskin-lined boots and two pairs of silk gloves under gauntlets, he would mount up. He could reckon on at least one, often two and occasionally three flights a day: each lasting for up to three hours.

They hunted whales in much the same way as the world's air arms were starting to hunt for submarines or for downed aviators. Search patterns known as 'box' or 'creeping line ahead' became second nature to the young pilot. Alan would come to know the difference between pods of fin whales and humpbacks, sperm whales or the rarer blue whales. He would also pass back the absence of sightings, since no news was often as valuable as good news.

He learned about the insidious dangers posed by icing. Although summer Antarctic conditions were often gin-clear, if he got caught out by fog or freezing rain squalls his rotor blades, engine intakes and any protuberances would quickly become coated or blocked with ice. At best this could erode the helicopter's performance but, if it affected vital intakes or broke off and hit the tail rotor, it could lead to a catastrophic failure.

Despite his best efforts to avoid it, on one occasion Alan discovered for himself the perils of rotor blade icing.

*I was out looking for whales one day, about 60 miles from the factory ship, navigating on dead reckoning via the Dalton computer [an aviator's circular slide rule] strapped to my knee. Then, in a matter of minutes, fog formed around me. I had no artificial horizon to help me stay upright so, to maintain visual contact with the sea, I had to quickly get down to the surface. I tried to recall where the icebergs had been and slowed to 30 to 35 knots.*

*I had a good idea where the factory ship was so I turned towards it. As ice from the fog slowly built on the rotor blades, my power requirement started to increase. I was too far away and too low to make VHF radio contact and too busy to stream the HF aerial. Although I knew that Joe would have the Challenger turn onto my last known bearing as soon as I missed a check-call, I also knew it might take over an hour to reach me. I seriously thought I might have to ditch and, without floats, started eyeing the Gibson Girl in the other seat. By now, even through my Frankenstein suit, I was beginning the feel the cold.*

*Suddenly I noticed something through the windscreen — nothing more than a different kind of light; a brighter glow — and pulled back a touch on the cyclic. I came to the hover just a few feet away from a huge wall of ice, disappearing into the fog on either side. I was face to face with an iceberg.*

*I sat there for a few moments and, once my heart-rate had subsided, tried to think of the best thing to do. I didn't know which way to go or which was the best way round the thing? How high was it? I could remember seeing a few slab bergs with sides about 50ft high. I didn't fancy trying to find out how long it was — they sometimes went on for a mile or more — so in the end I decided the best idea was to go upwards, and land on top of it.*

*I started to increase power and rotor rpm as I rose into the freezing fog. Almost immediately, I could feel the vibration increase and control response and rate-of-climb start to drop off. The blades were rapidly icing up. I climbed higher, with the berg wall still my only point of reference. Just as lift was beginning to disappear altogether, the intense brightness out of the cockpit suddenly vanished. I edged very slowly forward, made out a ledge of snow below me and, with my last gasp of power, settled onto it. The snow came right up to the door. Another 20ft and the only way would have been back down to the sea — and I wouldn't have been able to stop.*

*So there I was, sat on top of an iceberg. The helicopter seemed quite stable on the snow so I shut down — and then immediately wondered whether I'd done the right thing. Would it start again? But I needed to do something about the ice on my blades, so I waited for them to stop turning before stepping out onto the deep snow.*

*Stretching along the whole upper length of the two fabric-covered wooden blades, about three inches back from the leading edge, was a layer of knobbly rime ice nearly an inch thick. I imme-diately knew I had made the right decision to land. I had no tools with which to knock it off so I*

'Slab' bergs could extend for several miles. (Photo Andrew Healey)

*rocked the rotor head — some of it then fell off. After a few puffs on a cheroot I decided to try to work out the size of the berg, by walking in various directions, until I lost sight of the machine, and then retracing my footsteps in the snow. That didn't help very much — it was clearly a big one.*

*The HF wouldn't work without the aerial, so I put the Gibson Girl between my knees and turned the handle to transmit an SOS signal. I knew Joe would take a bearing off it and the* Olympic Challenger *would continue towards me, as fast as it safely could.*

*While I was preoccupied, the fog lifted a little, to reveal an enormous pinnacle of ice, with its peak still obscured by the fog, about a 'pitching wedge' distance ahead of the helicopter. I got back in the Hiller, lit another cheroot, and switched on the VHF. I couldn't afford to use it for long, for fear of draining the battery which I needed for one more engine start, but managed to pick up the* Challenger. *She was on her way at full speed.*

*Now able to relax, I sat back in the cockpit to wait for her. Then, without warning, there was a tremendous crack — like a 12-pound gun going off — followed by a rumble as the ice pinnacle toppled away from me, mercifully, into the sea. Another close call. The ship soon appeared, spotted me and manoeuvred its stern against the iceberg. Joe heaved a line to me and swung over a leather hammer and a broom, so that I could knock the ice off the rotor blades. I squeezed a final start from the battery and flew down to land on the flight deck.*

*I had a stiff drink that night, I can tell you. I hadn't been scared, but the exercise required an enormous amount of concentration. Looking back on the event gave me a real sense of accomplishment, but I also knew I had been very lucky.*

In the spring of 1952, Alan and Joe Soloy came back from their spell in the ice with cash in hand. Joe went back to California to settle his family's medical bills, and Alan pursued an idea that he felt could make the killing of whales both more humane and much more profitable. There was a great deal of competition in those sectors of the Antarctic where whaling was permitted. Using larger helicopters he planned not only to locate the creatures from the air, but also to hunt and kill them, leaving the tow-boats to recover the floating carcasses and deliver them to the factory ship.

*The process of killing these beautiful animals, which I witnessed at first hand on many occasions, was nothing less than barbaric. One harpoon was rarely enough and it sometimes took six of them to kill one blue whale, which often breathed its last with fountains of its blood spurting fifty feet into the air. I thought that if I could get close to the whale, I would be able to dispatch it cleanly, with one shot behind the lateral fins.*

Experiments in Germany had demonstrated that an electric current of enough amperage applied just behind the lateral fins, would electrocute a whale instantaneously. Alan also knew that whales, while their eyes and ears were above water, could not hear or see. The helicopter's ability to manoeuvre alongside a whale at close range, unseen and unheard, would almost guarantee a quick kill.

Earlier trials by Dutch company Hector Whaling had demonstrated the electric harpoons' worth but they had been seriously sabotaged by crews on the catchers, who cut the electric cables into pieces. This type of behaviour was typical of the deep-rooted opposition that the highly paid Norwegian gunners displayed, against anything that might make their jobs easier and, consequently, less valuable.

While working on his idea, Alan made plans to return for the next whaling season. He avoided dipping into his cash reserves by flying as a co-pilot for Airwork Ltd, out

Jack Woolley and Mickey Mörk.

Jack Woolley.

LN-ORG secured on deck. Note the blade clamps.

of Blackbushe Airport in Hampshire, and at weekends flew Seafires and Sea Furies for 1834 Naval Reserve Squadron, from RNAS Culham in Oxfordshire. Ted Wheeldon of Westland, with whom Alan was now back in favour following his altercation, was generous with flying hours on the company's WS51s and soon authorised him to sell their helicopters to the international whaling industry.

His first success was the sale of a WS51 Mk1A (G-AMRE, re-registered LN-ORG) – fitted with permanent doughnut-shaped floats around its wheels, HF radio, automatic direction finder and a life raft – to Norwegian whalers Melsom & Melsom. He won an operating contract as well so, in preparation for the 1952-1953 season, he trained a Norwegian pilot/navigator, Jan Kirkhorn, and took on two engineers, Einar (Mickey) Mörk and Jack Woolley.

Jack Woolley had been part of the team that designed the Canberra jet bomber and, until this point, had worked for aerial spraying contractors Pest Control Ltd. Alan needed a flight engineer, but also someone who could work on his electric harpoon idea. Jack's recruitment, on 5 June 1952, marked the beginning of a lifelong association with Alan Bristow.

Factory ship *Norhval* set off for the Antarctic in October. At about the same time, former Sub-Lt Alan Green also set off, with a Hiller 360 on a vessel belonging to a competitor – Anders Jahre. He went on to have an extremely successful season. Within a close-knit whaling community, where news travelled fast, the idea of using helicopters to spot whales was catching on.

The WS51's improved endurance and higher cruising speed greatly enlarged the area that could be covered by a search. Its fully-articulated main rotor was also less susceptible to icing. Excited with its performance during his second season, Alan left *Norhval* during its homeward voyage, at Cape Town, to sell more helicopters to the international whaling industry.

*Norhval* (with a whale on deck) and a catcher boat.

On his return to Somerset, he rented four old Nissen huts and a hangar from the Royal Navy at Henstridge Airfield in Somerset, a former satellite field to the nearby Yeovilton air station. On 6 June 1953, he formed a company – Air Whaling Ltd – to take on new contracts, handle the sales of the helicopters and train the crews to operate them. He talked Jack Woolley into becoming technical director and asked George Fry, who he had first met atop the Olympia building and who had been helping Alan with his personal accounts, to serve as part-time financial director. Soon after, pilot Alan Green, fresh from Anders Jahre, completed the embryonic team as operations director.

Over the next two years Jack would design and build a lightweight harpoon gun that could be fired by a crewman in the back of a helicopter. He also worked on a device for helping the less pliable electric cable run freely off its drum, once the harpoon had been fired. To Alan's design he produced a lance device, known as a steel bodkin, with a hollow shaft to carry both current to electrocute the whale and gas to inflate the carcass. He also designed a quick-release coupling that would enable the helicopter to break free from the whale if, were the first shot not fatal, it made an abrupt dive.

Alan asked engineer Yasha Shapiro to design a generator that would be powerful enough, yet light enough to be fitted in the cabin of the WS55. This new helicopter, another Westland-built Sikorsky design with an R1340 Wasp piston engine, had a larger cabin in which a crewman could handle a harpoon launcher.

He persuaded Siemens to produce a conductor reliable enough to run, inside the insulated cable, to the harpoon head. He also bought a set of precision machine tools, with which Jack could develop his engineering capacity. Despite all this effort, however, they were nowhere near a position where they could demonstrate a proven system to the whaling industry. To maintain a cash-flow, there was more whale-spotting to be done.

In the autumn of 1953, Green, Woolley, Kirkhorn, Mörk and two other Norwegians left once more for the Antarctic, again for Melsom & Melsom and this time flying a WS55. Alan stayed behind to market the new company. The bigger helicopter made even longer flights practical and, until it was lost in an accident, was proving a great success. Fortunately the crew, Kirkhorn and Mörk, were uninjured. Notwithstanding this incident, by now several of the big whaling companies were interested in using them for ice reconnaissance, as well as for spotting whales.

Back home in 1954, Air Whaling faced a hectic summer of training crews, setting up stores inventories and manufacturing ground equipment. Alan persuaded the Netherlands Whaling Company to fund his machine shop, which would enable Jack Woolley to complete work on the 'humane whale killer'. Alan sold four new WS55s (G-ANJS, G-ANJH, G-ANJT and G-ANJV) to Scottish whalers Christian Salvesen.

This time Alan decided they should fly in crews of two: one to fly and plot position; the other to look out for whales. New pilots were required and Spencer Allen, Bill Loftus, Earl Milburn, Ron Osborne, Ralph Seaton, Bob Smith, and Dave Thrippleton joined John Cameron and Clive Wright on the payroll. They were supported by engineers hired from Westland and Alastair Gordon, an engineer and design draughtsman with Bristol Aircraft who had qualified as a pilot during National Service. He subsequently flew with Alan Bristow as a co-pilot, as a captain in his own right and, over a 30-year career with BHL, rose to the position of operations director. Kay Sealby was also taken on, as Alan's first secretary.

For the 1954-1955 season they flew the four helicopters from two Christian Salvesen factory ships – *Southern Harvester* and *Southern Venturer* – with Alan in charge of the first pair and Green the second.

Alan Green (left) with Clive Wright. (Express Newspapers)

Clive Wright (left) and Earl Milburn share a bar of chocolate.

Landing on. (*Newcastle Chronicle*)

Clive Wright (left) with Bob Smith of Salvesen.

Air Whaling earned commission for the sale of the four Salvesen WS55s, plus others delivered to the Netherlands Whaling Company, and management fees for running the Christian Salvesen contract. With six or seven machines now in operation, the concept of using helicopters in whaling was beginning to show results, if not in the way that Alan had been hoping.

As if to confirm his fears, the 1954-1955 season was only marginally successful, even with four machines operating at increased ranges. He knew it was purely a matter of finding enough whales of a suitable size and the failure convinced Alan that the future, more than ever, lay in killing whales from his helicopters.

Another disappointment presented itself when four of the pilots – Loftus, Osborne, Smith and Seaton – left to join Christian Salvesen, which was setting up its own spotting crew at Staverton Airport, near Gloucester. That business continued until 1961.

> *Throughout this period Jack and I had been working on our humane whale killer. We were trying to find a lightweight, virtually recoilless launcher that we could mount in the doorway of the WS55 and that would be accurate to about 100 yards. George Fry had met Colonel Stewart*

*Blacker, who had invented the recoilless PIAT (projector infantry anti-tank) missile launcher of World War 2 fame. I went to see him at his house near Petersfield and we fired off a few of them into earth bunkers in a nearby field. At 100 yards Blacker could hit a 2ft-diameter target with his PIAT and, after a bit of practice, I managed that eight out of ten times. I persuaded him to sell me a launcher and the patents for £1000.*

In readiness for what would have been its fifth season, the Air Whaling team demonstrated its new system to three executives from the Netherlands Whaling Co. over Weymouth Bay. Alan knew that the company was building a new factory ship – the *Willem Barendsz II* – and he wanted the business. He flew the helicopter with Blacker manning the gun, mounted on a tripod in the doorway of the WS55, and Alan Green drove a speedboat, carrying the five Dutchmen and towing a series of fifty-gallon oil drums, mounted on pontoons.

Each time Blacker fired, Green heard a muffled explosion from the helicopter and, as the missile struck home behind them, a clanging impact. Bristow hovered alongside and Blacker fired nine more missiles. Three narrowly missed as the drum rolled wildly in the boat's wake. The other six were direct hits and the last one knocked the drum from its mounting and straight down to the seabed.

At the debriefing back at Henstridge, Alan Bristow could hardly contain himself.

*Gentlemen, if that drum had been a whale you would have been £2,000 richer after the first shot, and would have killed six more whales in the next ten minutes. All that from two men and one helicopter.*

*Think of how many you could get if you sent a whole fleet of helicopters, equipped with weapons like this, into the Antarctic. They would kill whales more humanely and in greater numbers than all the fleets in the world put together.*

*Willem Barendsz II.*

First overhaul at Henstridge.

The Dutchmen were greatly impressed with the manoeuvrability of the helicopter and the accuracy of the harpoon, which they had seen so effortlessly fired from its cabin door. Before they had left for Amsterdam, Alan had sold them the rights for the gun and harpoon, four WS55s to go on the back of the *Willem Barendsz II* and a management contract to operate them during the 1955-1956 season.

Henstridge was ready to go into overdrive that spring and Westland had been put on standby. Then, out of the blue, came a fatal blow. The International Whaling Commission in Sandefjord, Norway, had decided to reclassify flying machines that were fitted with harpoons, as whale-catchers in their own right. No operator would want to replace his fleet of boats with a similar number of expensive helicopters – and at the same time make his fleet of catchers and their crews redundant – so Air Whaling's business plan was immediately dead in the water. Alan could see the IWC was protecting its members' interests. 'They realised that hunting by helicopter was so efficient that it would put a lot of their gunners, who were the captains and boat-owners as well, out of work. So they put the lid on it.'

Although Air Whaling had been paid handsomely for its harpoon patent, it suddenly had no work and no obvious prospects. Alan was frustrated. 'We have a good bunch of people and we have ideas. All we need now are customers.'

It was Jean Bristow who came up with a suggestion which changed everyone's lives. 'Why don't you switch from whale oil to mineral oil?'

## CHAPTER THREE

# WORLDWIDE OR NOTHING

By the time his air whaling business had come to an unexpected halt, in the spring of 1955, Alan Bristow's company assets consisted of the Nissen huts and hangar at Henstridge – known as the H block – six good machine tools and the skills of Woolley, Fry, Gordon, Green, Kay Sealby and himself. The other pilots had been laid off and found other jobs.

The Navy had by now departed Henstridge for good, taking the electricity supply along with it. To get round this problem, Woolley drove down to Portsmouth in search of a diesel generator. Unfortunately the only one he could find, an ex-Navy frigate engine, was so big that it needed one major effort to get it out to the airfield, followed by another to get it under cover. Once in operation at Henstridge it provided far too much energy for the small business' modest needs so, to absorb the excess and prevent it overheating, twenty domestic heaters were kept going at full blast in the hangar.

George Fry said the generator put out enough energy to centrally heat Somerset. As he was often the last man out at night, he regularly had to turn the thing off, and did not relish the prospect. 'The only way was to reach a hand into the maw of the thumping beast, twist it round a couple of corners, and then screw down a valve. Whereupon of course everything went pitch black.'

The two remaining pilots turned their skills to charter work. Alan Green flew a WS51 (the unfortunately registered G-ANAL) on publicity stunts for the *London Evening Standard*, and even bulk-delivered newspapers, until he was caught low-flying and reprimanded (see *The Book of Igor*, written at the time, in the Appendix). Bristow rented another WS51 to fly with Jack Woolley to the Channel Island of Sark, where he demonstrated its versatility to the resident Dame.

On Jean's suggestion, Bristow soon got on the phone to Shell Oil. He made contact with the renowned Douglas Bader who, by now, had retired from the RAF and become the first managing director of Shell Aircraft. Supported by a small team in a London office, he was ultimately responsible for the safety of any aircraft that

The *Evening Standard*'s WS51. (Agusta Westland)

carried the oil company's personnel on duty, wherever in the world they might be. He was the first leader of a unit that would soon become identified with the highest standards of flight safety.

By sheer coincidence, Bader had just been handed a requirement to support a number of Shell exploration rigs some forty-five miles off Doha, part of the Sheikhdom of Qatar in the Persian Gulf. A boat service was taking too long to get out to them and was unreliable. Bad weather also disrupted up to 50% of the trips and helicopters were being considered. The two men hit it off from the start and Bader soon agreed the framework of a contract, whereby Shell would provide the helicopters and Bristow would manage the operation and supply the crews. Bader asked him to fly out the next day with his deputy, Roy Snodgrass, to locate a base for the new operation.

Bristow was so elated to get this new business that, as Jack Woolley recalls, he practically ran up the wall of his office back at Henstridge. He called everyone in, pointed to a map on the wall and exclaimed, 'That's the world – and we're going to fly all over it.'

Bristow's infectious enthusiasm was balanced by cold commonsense from his colleagues. Before the Shell contract was finalised George Fry had mused, 'do you think they can afford the luxury of your helicopters?' Bristow later said that his question

Doha, 1955.

became the yardstick against which he assessed the potential of every future business opportunity. 'It brought home to me the highly specialised nature of the service we were trying to sell. It was not long before I came to appreciate the limited number of markets that could support such an expensive and specialised piece of equipment. In order to survive, we would have to look for work anywhere in the world.'

A new company, Bristow Helicopters Ltd (BHL), was formed. Bristow and Snodgrass soon found a plot of desert on the coast of Qatar. It was close to the shoreline so that, should an engine fail on take-off, the float-equipped helicopters could land on calm waters in front of the hangar. Bader bought two WS55 Whirlwinds (G-AODA and G-AODB) from Westland and Bristow supplied the crews – himself and Alan Green, with Earl Milburn and Alastair Gordon as co-pilots – and recruited engineers. After a forty-three-hour ferry flight through France, Italy, Greece, Cyprus and down the Syria/Iraq pipeline, the helicopters arrived in Doha – on the same day as a Transair DC3, carrying all the spares and support equipment.

Flight familiarisation in Doha started with the pilots getting used to the power limitations caused by the hot and humid environment. With its heavy piston engine, the performance of the WS55 was marginal in high temperature and nil wind conditions. They found that payload had to be reduced to five passengers and, to make the most of the cooler conditions, night flying soon became routine. They practised engine-off landings onto the water without hydraulic assistance, a skill that required a certain amount of brute strength.

The new service quickly established itself as a reliable and swift alternative to the boats. Whereas the boats struggled to reach the rig in any bad weather, the helicopters were stopped by the conditions only once in six months. During a typical month, a hundred flights totalling eighty-eight hours moved 436 passengers and 16,000lb of freight. They carried men, tools, spare parts and groceries. They also brought out sick and injured workers – it was a tremendous boost to oil workers' morale to know that hospital treatment was now only half an hour's flight away.

Not that there weren't challenges to overcome; particularly with keeping the machines serviceable. Sand caused severe erosion to the blades, in spite of leading-edge protection by a new protective tape from 3M, and engine air filters had to be frequently changed. The temperature and salt-laden humidity meant that the pilots had to watch their performance margins, and so to make as much use of the ground cushion as they could, they perfected very shallow approaches to the helidecks. The engineers also made careful checks for airframe and engine corrosion.

Later that year disaster struck. A sudden squall blew up around a jack-up drilling rig while Alan Green's helicopter was on the pad. In minutes, the structure began to break up beneath him and Green took off as soon as he could, with eight technicians packed aboard. They were carried safely ashore but, before he could return, the rig collapsed and twenty-two oil workers were drowned.

Rig off Das.

A Bristow Widgeon. (Photo Agusta Westland)

In 1957 BHL won a competitive tender from BP to operate off Das, a small island some seventy miles off Qatar. This time, and for the first time, the company bought its own helicopters. Initially the two Widgeons (G-AOZD and G-AOZE) – converted WS51s with a two-seat cockpit – were required to fly only essential spares and key executives to the rigs, but such was the high standard of availability achieved by Bill Petrie – a recent arrival from BEA Helicopters – and his team of engineers, that BP decided to transfer the entire rig crews by helicopter instead of by boat. In 1959 the contract was expanded to include two Whirlwinds (G-APWM and G-APWN).

The company would continue to operate in this area of the Middle East for the next twenty years and, when the facilities were put in place, decamped to the international airport at Abu Dhabi. However one aircraft, usually a Whirlwind, would always be based on Das Island and maintained by the resident crew. Between Das and the mainland were the two main oilfields, Zakum and Umm Schaif.

In October 1957, with the Doha and Das operations in full swing, BHL started flying on seismic support duties in Iran, a contract won against stiff opposition from hungry US competition. Earl Milburn and Alastair Gordon, again supported by

Das Island, 1960.

The delivery of the first WS55 to Das Island. Bill Petrie is in front of the nose and Clive Wright is at the far right.

Das Island.

Loading freight at Das.
(Photo Guy Gravett)

A Widgeon at Das Island, 1958.

Approach to the *Adma Enterprise* drilling rig, 1957. (Photo BP)

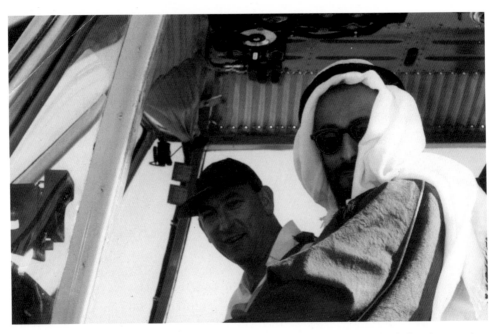

Alan Bristow flies Sheikh Shakhbut bin Sultan, Ruler of Abu Dhabi, to the mobile drilling barge *Adma Enterprise* off Das Island, December 1957.

At a rig off Das Island. (Photo Andrew T. Paton)

Bill Petrie, flew crews of explosives experts along survey lines, where they set charges with which to measure the structure of the sub-surface layers. Two Whirlwinds were flown around Gach Saran and Mas el Suliven (about 100km in from the coast) and at the Khori Mond structure near Bushire. Bristow recalls the Whirlwinds were 'thoroughly unsuitable machines, because of power limitations at altitude. It was probably the most difficult flying we had ever done. As well as the lack of power in hot and high conditions, we had to contend with severe and unpredictable turbulence.'

The company was soon approached by the Shah, who needed to travel around Iran to supervise his land reform policy. French engineer Jean Dennel was hired by Alan Bristow to maintain a solitary Alouette 2, to be flown by compatriot Jacques Castaigne, in support of an Italian consultancy in the eastern province of Baluchistan. Seven months later, Jacques was relieved by ex-Navy pilot Ian Clark and the pair continued with high-altitude work in the Zagros mountains.

The service, together with the personal contact it involved, put BHL in pole position when it came to pitching for further business. Indeed the Shah's younger sister, Princess Fatima, became a partner in the Iranian operation.

A year later BHL won a three-year contract with Iran Pan American Oil to support drilling operations offshore at Khosrovabad, south-east of Basra. For this job BHL sent out three float-equipped Whirlwinds and the crews to go with them.

The caption on this photograph reads 'One more word out of you, [Ken] Bradley, and you'll get no f*****g cost-of-living allowance at all!' Das Island, late fifties.

Seismic survey, Gach Saran, 1960-1961.

Alan Bristow flew this WS55-1 from Khosrovabad to Kharg Island in March 1959. (Photo Westland Aircraft)

Between then and the 1979 revolution, which would initiate one of the most famous operations in the company's history, the operation expanded to one of more than twenty helicopters, supported by over 300 people.

Summer conditions in the marshy Shatt al Arab delta area were extremely hot and the crews took every opportunity to cool down. Indeed some of the pilots got into the habit of taking off their life jackets, in-flight, as soon as they went 'feet dry' over the coast. Phil Sipeck was a particularly lanky pilot who, while wrestling with his own preserver, managed to knock off both magneto switches on the overhead console. That mistake immediately shut down his engine as well.

The aircraft sank rapidly and Sipeck, still struggling with the life jacket but now with rather more urgency, was lucky to survive the near-vertical impact into the coastal swamp. The helicopter, however, did not. The crestfallen aviator was quickly winched out but immediately dispatched, in another helicopter, to winch down Bill Petrie so that he could assess how to recover the wreck. The fact that the tide was starting to come in leant added urgency to the operation.

It was clear that the aircraft would have to be dismantled and lifted out, piece by piece, to be landed above the high-water mark. This was only a few minutes' flight away and, once a team including Petrie and fellow-engineer Jean Dennel went to work, the operation went smoothly. Finally only the tail cone was left, and Petrie attached it to the helicopter's cargo hook. Sipeck flew it inshore and then returned

Recovery from the Shatt al Arab delta.

to pick up Petrie on the winch. Jean Dennel was briefed to give basic conning instructions, in his heavy French accent, from the cabin. Jean recalls:

*The winch motor was extremely slow so we had arranged that, as I was lifting Bill, Phil would climb vertically to gain extra height, before transitioning into forward flight and turning towards the landing site. Bill hooked himself on and I told Phil to go 'up, up, up'. Unfortunately he didn't go 'up, up, up' anything like far enough, and poor Bill was dragged through the tops of the palm trees, all the way back to land. When we landed Bill released himself from the winch and climbed into the cabin, covered in deep cuts from the sharp palm leaves.*

Jean and Phil blamed each other for misunderstanding the brief. Bill, who had a particularly slow-burning fuse, didn't believe either of them and made his displeasure clear. 'Anyway', says Jean, 'by then we were all too tired to make much of a fuss.'

In September 1957, an opportunity arose to expand into South America. Shell Aircraft invited tenders for an operation to support geological field parties searching for signs of oil under the Bolivian riverbeds, in the eastern foothills of the Andes. Uniquely, one of the tendering conditions for the contract was to show proof of ownership of the proposed helicopters, so Bristow and George Fry scoured the market for short-term hire-purchase deals. They found one with Lombard Finance but still had to find £25,000 – so everyone in the company put their own savings up as collateral. Bill Petrie, for one, did so without telling his wife. It was by no means certain that they would get the contract and if they failed, all would have been lost. After a tense two weeks, their faith was rewarded.

Soon two Bell 47G1s (VR-BAT and VR-BAW) were on their way to Bolivia inside a DC4. Alan Bristow, Alan Green, Jacques Castaigne and Marcel Avon went over to fly them and Bill Petrie, Neil Leppard and 'Robbie' Robinson supported them in the field. Shortly afterwards came another contract, this time from a Standard Oil subsidiary, to carry out similar operations using another two more Bell G2s (VR-BBA and VR-BBB). Earl Milburn and Alastair Gordon took over this flying operation, with new pilots relieving them in the Gulf. Bristow recalls:

*We would fly the geologists out from base camp at first light and back at dusk. We never knew quite where we would be going until the last minute. The pilot often had to work with the scientist and help him carry the rock samples, so it was physically demanding work. We moved camp every ten days or so, which involved moving everything and everyone by helicopter. The flying was often over dense jungle and we would frequently have to make up to 30 landings – on rough terrain in small clearings – during an average two-hour flight. I learned a lot about jungle flying from Marcel Avon. He would note the colour of the trees in a given area and plot their position relative to a landmark such as a river bend or rocky outcrop. We would transfer the information to our own charts – Bolivian ones were useless but ours weren't much better – and it helped us find our way around a comparatively featureless landscape.*

*Operating conditions at the beginning of the Bolivian operations were extremely primitive. As we gained experience it became clear that we needed much better maintenance facilities, if we were to provide the high degree of aircraft availability that our customers needed. As part of our subsequent contract bids, I always insisted on hangarage for the helicopters. I didn't want our engineers to work in the open, unless in an emergency.*

Bill Petrie up to his knees in Iranian mud.

55

Bell 47G2.

> *To achieve this, we built wooden hangar and workshop facilities that could be dismantled and transferred between jungle base camps. They were capable of carrying out all necessary mainte-nance up to 'C III' requirements. For Check IVs and major overhauls, we built and equipped an inspection and overhaul shop in Cochabamba, a large town just to the east of the Andes.*

Bill Petrie, by now a veteran of service overseas, earned a reputation for trying to make life bearable in the most unlikely of environments. After on several occasions finding himself stranded in the middle of the Bolivian jungle, with a small party of geologists and Indian bearers for company, he decided that the only thing that would make the situation tolerable would be a fully fitted bathroom suite.

Bill was appalled at the living conditions everyone seemed prepared to accept.

> *They'd just chop down some saplings, throw a tarp over them, and that was it. Not surprisingly, they got bitten to death – Bolivia was full of things that either flew and bit or crawled and bit. We usually camped on the banks of a river and the only hygiene regulations in force were that you washed up-stream and crapped down-stream.*
>
> *First chance I got, I converted a 45-gallon drum into a shower. The local Amerindians seemed to enjoy helping me and so I thought I'd go a bit further. Next time I was in La Paz, I bought a shower rose and lavatory seat. Everybody laughed at me. I dug a hole, cut down some saplings to go over the top, screwed the toilet roll holder into a bit of wood, and that was that. The idea soon caught on and, before you knew it, everyone was building their own bathroom facilities.*

Petrie was pleased with his individual brand of 'white man's magic'. However he soon discovered that, when it came to understanding the jungle, the locals – even without the aid of double-ply soft toilet paper – could still teach him a thing or two.

*Moving camp one day we came to a site where the ground was very wet, with the exception of one slightly higher patch. We immediately picked this dry area, pitched our tents and spent the rest of the afternoon watching the Amerindians put in a lot of effort, cutting wood and building platforms on the soggy ground. Of course it soon rained and the whole area flooded – and every bloody snake in creation slithered up on to our bit of dry ground! It didn't take us long to join the locals in the bog.*

Snakes were not the only problems in Bolivia. Some of the more remote Indian tribes could prove dangerous as well. Much of the Bolivian operation involved flying into areas where the Amerindians had never seen a white man before, let alone a helicopter. Clearings had to be cut in the rainforest for the helicopters to land and this was achieved by suspending an Amerindian, armed with chainsaw and machete, on a rope ladder from a Bell 47. He would disappear into the canopy with the greatest incentive to work ever devised – he could not be pulled out again until the clearing was finished. The forest cover was so thick that, at first, they could not be seen at all.

One of these clearing expeditions ended in violent tragedy. Bill remembers:

*The cutters were attacked by another tribe. I flew out there to see what had happened. Two of our cutters had been killed and one had an arrow clean through his chest. He couldn't get through the little door in the bubble of the Bell 47, so I cut off the front and back of the arrow and we managed to get him into the aircraft. He couldn't lean back against the seat so we packed him*

Surveying in Bolivia, 1957.

Major surgery in Bolivia.

*with all sorts of stuff – cigarette packets, bags of rice – to make him a bit more comfortable, and then flew him off to hospital. We discovered that the problem had arisen because nobody had contacted this other tribe in advance, and our cutters hadn't realised that they were encroaching on their territory. Within a couple of weeks it was all sorted out. If we wanted clearings it was fine by them, as long as we gave them some rice. It really was fascinating to be amongst these people.*

The frontier aspects of Third World life were not confined to the jungle and its inhabitants. They also extended to local flying practices. The Bolivians had a novel way of air-freighting meat, which required a brand of airmanship that impressed Petrie.

*Cattle were driven to the airport, slaughtered, butchered and then loaded on to B17s or Liberators, and then flown to the main cities. The system of payment was by kilo on arrival rather than what they loaded before take-off. So they packed the aircraft with as much meat as it would hold, and headed for the lowest pass. If that was blocked by low cloud they'd throw out enough meat to enable them to climb and clear the next lowest pass. They sometimes had to go as high as 24,000 feet, way above the B17's ceiling, in order to get to La Paz. Some of those Bolivian pilots knew the mountains like the back of their hands and you were far better off with them, than some of the 'gringos' who used to come down to fly the old WWII bombers. One of them put us down on what he thought was an airstrip. It turned out to be a bloody big cow patch. The Bolivians just never got lost.*

At La Paz one day, while trying to reach Cochabamba, George Fry encountered one of these aviators after discovering that the local airline was on strike.

*I had to find a way of covering the final 250 miles and the train took 48 hours, so that wasn't an option. Someone suggested I get in touch with Kiko, a Bolivian who owned a clapped-out old DC4. He ran a freight service and might be persuaded to take me.*

*I walked over to the other side of the airport to find Kiko, standing by his battered old crate and smoking a big cigar, and asked him if he could take me to Cochabamba. 'Sure,' he said. 'When do you want to go?' 'Well, now,' I said. 'OK, let's go now,' he said. 'I'm all loaded up.' I climbed into the jump seat and saw that the cargo bay was packed with fencing posts, coils of barbed wire and about 20 sheep under a net. 'You get heart trouble?' asked Kiko. 'No,' I said. 'That's good,' he said. 'We'll be up at 18,000ft and I ain't got oxygen.'*

*We took off and, about half an hour later, I noticed that the compass needle was swinging wildly. I pointed this out to Kiko and he said not to worry. 'Compass never works,' he said. 'All these little hills are full of iron.' By this time we were flying over a lunar landscape, with boulders the size of houses. I said, 'Well, thank goodness we've got a radio.' 'Radio? Oh, radio never works. All these little hills are full of iron.' 'Well I hope you know the way.' 'Oh sure,' said Kiko. Then, after a pause, 'I theenk'.*

*And of course we made it. Cochabamba lies in the middle of a horseshoe of mountains. There's just one way in and the landing requires a pretty sharp left-hand turn onto short finals. He brought the big DC4 in and touched it down like a feather. Brilliant pilot, as it turned out.*

Towards the end of his time in Bolivia, Alan Green landed in an uninhabited area and, knowing it was safe to leave the helicopter unguarded, joined one of the geologists in his search for samples. When they returned, the helicopter looked as though it had changed colour to deep violet and seemed to be quivering slightly – even though the engine was switched off.

As they approached the helicopter, bits of it appeared to flake off and float into the sky. They then realised what the bits were. 'Butterflies,' gasped the geologist. 'Millions of them!' They were everywhere – in the cockpit, on the seats, on the rotor blades – covering every inch of metal and shimmering in the light. Green had to dust them from his seat before he could sit down, and some were still in position as the rotors engaged. As Green later recalled, 'it was an amazing sight'.

Word of another Bolivian contract soon reached Bristow's ears and he flew to Cochabamba to bid for it. He found himself in a big room with executives from Amoseas and representatives from his main competition – US-based operators such as Petroleum Helicopters (PHI), Columbia, Carson, Keystone and Evergreen.

After listening to a short brief – the job involved seismic and geophysical support flying, and they would have to provide most of their own tents and domestic equipment – they were asked how soon they could have their helicopters in position. Bristow was first in line and said 'seven days, sir'. The other bidders looked at each other. 'How do you plan to do that?' asked the Amoseas executive. 'Inside a DC4, straight into the nearest airfield.' After that, of course, everyone else said 'seven days' as well.

Then they were asked to give their price for doing the job, based on an hourly flying rate. This time, thankfully, the executive started at the other end of the line so, by the time he came to Bristow, the Englishman had had time to think. 'I can't tender for this contract on this basis, sir, because neither of us know how much we're going to fly. Furthermore, I need an assurance of a basic minimum income, for when my pilots are grounded because of bad weather. Otherwise I'm not covering my costs.'

This caught the Amoseas man's attention and Bristow was asked how *he* would bid for it. 'I'd make an establishment charge, to cover time when we're not flying for any reason, and a reduced hourly rate on top.' 'How much would that be then?' 'Well I need to know roughly how many flying hours are involved. Otherwise this is just a fishing expedition.'

When the meeting was over, the oil man told everyone he'd let them know. Bristow was immediately grabbed by one operator's rep and accused, in effect, of sharp practice. 'But how on earth could we work out an hourly rate, when he didn't know how much we were going to fly and we needed to provide almost everything ourselves?' The executive agreed he didn't want to work on that basis either, but had not been prepared to make a stand at the meeting himself.

*The next day Alan Green and I went back and sat down in the office with a couple of legal types, to work out a contract based on what I had suggested. Almost immediately one of the other bidders got in touch and told me he'd like to buy me out. I countered that I'd rather buy him! Meanwhile the two Bell 47s arrived in Cochabamba as promised and, two days later, were earning their keep in Todos Santos.*

Ultimately the Bolivian adventure turned out to be a failure – at least in terms of its oil potential. Apart from the odd tantalising glimpse from a wildcat well, the exploration teams did not find what they were looking for and the contracts were wound up in 1962. The BHL team, who had come to love the country and several of whom married local girls, shared the oil men's disappointment but they had the huge consolation of knowing that their helicopters had more than earned their keep. They had proved their worth in the most inhospitable of environments.

By about this time Alan Bristow had made the decision to stop flying. 'We were being pulled in several directions at once', he said at the time, 'and someone had to keep a hand on the tiller.' It turned out to be a perceptive move. His personal reputation, both for winning new business and for treating his staff fairly, was growing and people were keen to work for him. They also gave of their best once they did. 'He was a charismatic leader who was accessible to anyone on the payroll – from chief pilot to hangar sweeper,' recalls George Fry. 'He inspired loyalty and I think most of the men would have done anything for him.'

The timing was also right because, by the end of the fifties, the groundwork for future expansion of BHL had been laid. Jack Woolley is certain that standards established right at the beginning of the company's life – that it would maintain best engineering practices, that it would always support operations with properly qualified engineers and that it would never use 'pirated' spares – gave it a solid basis from which to grow. 'We were nearly all ex-servicemen who had learned how to stick by the rules. We became known for the quality of our service and, in particular, earned a reputation for turning up on time and being ready to start work on schedule. This became a golden rule for BHL crews and one which, for a long time, marked us out from the competition.'

The procedures that Jack set up at Henstridge, for the maintenance and overhaul of airframes and major components required for Air Registration Board approval, and essential for operating helicopters in the public transport category, still hold good today. Together with maintenance schedules and historical technical records, they were adhered to no matter what foreign registration the helicopters were operating under. This allowed for flexibility when moving aircraft from one foreign country to another.

Alan Bristow summed up how they managed to win, and keep, an ever-increasing level of business:

> *Contacts. I made and cultivated as many as I could. Presidents of oil companies, cabinet ministers and rebels who might become cabinet ministers; civil servants who weave all the red tape and lawyers who think they know how to cut it. You've got to know how much it costs to operate each type of helicopter and be prepared to fly it anywhere on this earth, at any time of the day or night, to take on anything that's worth doing.*
>
> *And when you get the job, perhaps in the middle of nowhere, the secret is to employ men you trust. I'd fire a pilot on the spot if I discovered he touched a beer during a working day, even if he and his helicopter were sitting in the middle of the jungle, a hundred miles from anywhere. They may call us bush pilots but first, last and always, we are professional pilots. The only bush around us comes with the scenery.*

This philosophy went down very well with Bristow customers, and the money started to roll in.

A Bristow Widgeon at Battersea Heliport.

Widgeon over the River Thames, 1961. (Photo John Gay)

CHAPTER FOUR

# GROWTH OF AN OPERATOR

In 1958 the taxman started to take an interest in Bristow Helicopters. When Alan Bristow and George Fry had been costing up the Middle East and South America contracts, they arranged that they would, in Fry's words, 'generate some pretty good profit margins'.

*But we wanted to expand [explains Fry]. To do that we needed to buy more helicopters and so we invested all our profits in them. After several meetings with tax counsel in London, it was eventually decided to form a subsidiary company in Bermuda to run our operations.*

*At the time we were also having problems in a number of countries, with the British licences that all our pilots and engineers held. In some areas of the world, the UK still had to deal with its post-colonial legacy and was not always popular. Even in those days, we also had to comply with a great many more flying regulations than most. Coincidentally, we had formed friendly relations with the Bermudan aviation authority and, in particular, its director of civil aviation, Wing Commander Mo Ware. So we went to Bermuda.*

*I flew out first in April 1958 and set up a new company, Bristow Helicopters (Bermuda) Ltd, which paved the way for several of our helicopters and licences to be transferred to the Bermudan register. All the Bolivia and Iran-based aircraft were re-registered in this way. A year later we also set up a leasing company, Helicopter Rentals. However the UK tax authorities became increasingly restless, at one point issuing a Surtax Direction Order, and we were eventually advised that the only way to legitimately avoid the liability would be for Alan himself to leave the country.*

So Alan followed Fry out to Bermuda and was followed by Kay Sealby. He stuck it out for six months but everyone quickly realised that it made no sense, for the boss of a growing business to be trying to run it at arm's length from half-way across the Atlantic. As it turned out, he spent most of his time away from the island anyway. He door-stepped as many of the US oil companies as he could find and preached the gospel of the helicopter as something they had to have, both for their offshore operations and for overcoming difficult terrain. By October he was back in the UK: both he and the company resigned to meeting their obligations to the Exchequer.

While he was in Bermuda, however, Alan met Freddie Laker. As he was for much of his working life, the entrepreneur was either buying or running an airline. Bristow remembers arriving home from New York, one Friday evening, to find a note from Jean saying she had gone to a cocktail party at the home of Air Commodore 'Taffy' Powell. Taffy had founded an airline – Eagle Airways – and Laker was interested in it.

When Alan arrived the party had been in full swing for some time and many of the guests were well-lubricated. The story goes that Laker tottered over to Bristow and poked him in the stomach. 'You're Alan Bristow. I want to do a deal with you.' Although Bristow had never met Laker, he remembered that an acquaintance had identified him as a rising star in the airline business. 'We can do that tomorrow, Freddie, when you're sober.' 'No. I'm going back to England tomorrow.' At this point he poked Bristow in the stomach once more. His short temper already deserting him, Alan retorted: 'You do that to me again and I'll flatten you. If you want to talk to me – call me in the morning.' With that he turned on his heel, left the party and went home to bed.

Early next morning the telephone rang, and Laker suggested that their two families went fishing together before his flight home. Once on the water, he told Bristow that he wanted to buy his business.

'Freddie, you don't have enough money,' he replied. Laker explained he was negotiating on behalf of Myles (later Sir Myles) Wyatt who was Chairman of Airwork Ltd. The business was trying to expand and BHL, by now a flourishing business with international operations involving over a dozen helicopters and over 100 employees, would add an extra dimension to Airwork's portfolio.

BHL, on the other hand, was always strapped for cash. Having made the strategic decision to buy rather than lease its helicopters, writing them off in the books over comparatively short periods, the company needed capital to buy them. Then, of course, it needed to pay it back. 'The advantage of taking the purchasing route', explains Fry, 'is at the end of it all you've got a helicopter, which you hope will remain an asset over many years. It's when you get the next job that you start turning a profit.' The pair chose their airframes well: one of the original Bolivian B47Gs was eventually sold forty years later. But the strategy did not help the balance of the company's current account.

The fishing trip negotiations went no further. Laker returned to the UK and Bristow, ready to go home as well, called George Fry and said that they ought to talk to him. 'He's quite a character and says he wants to buy the business.'

'What did you tell him?'
'I told him he didn't have enough money.'
'Well that was the right answer.'
'Maybe George, but I don't want to spend the rest of my life in Bermuda. Go and talk to him and see if he means it.'

Fry went to see both Laker and Wyatt in London. Bristow flew back to the UK and, with Fry, worked out what they thought the company was worth. They had several meetings with Laker and Wyatt but could not agree on a price. In a last ditch effort to reach an agreement, Wyatt suggested that Bristow and Laker should have lunch together and try to thrash something out.

Alan remembers the occasion well.

*We met at Simpsons of Piccadilly. George Fry was with me and Laker had his financial advisor, George Carroll. We were unable to agree a price as neither of us would budge. If I remember correctly the gap was £60,000: a substantial sum in those days. In the end Freddie said, 'let's toss for it!'*

*George kicked me under the table as if to say, 'don't you dare', and I said to Freddie, 'don't be daft'. Freddie said, 'come on, we'll never agree otherwise', and he tossed a coin and I won.*

*We went on eating as if nothing had happened. Later that afternoon we went back to see Myles Wyatt and drew up Heads of Agreement. When they were finished Freddie said to me: 'You're a lucky bugger, you know, Alan.'*

*'Considering some of the things I've done', I replied, 'I'm lucky to be alive!'*

*'Will you do me a favour? Buy me a racehorse. There's this little filly I fancy.'*

*I didn't ask how much and thought, there goes my 60 grand, but I said yes I would. He bought the horse and, when I asked him how much it was, he said '£1,400.'*

*So that was a good day's work, one way or another.*

Bristow himself made over half a million pounds on the deal. His companies, Bristow Helicopters (Eastern), Bristow Helicopters, Bristow Helicopters (Bermuda) and Helicopter Rentals, duly became subsidiaries of Airwork. In late 1959 they left Henstridge and moved to Redhill aerodrome in Surrey, just north of London's Gatwick Airport. A year later George Fry left his accountancy firm for good and joined BHL as full-time financial director and general manager. He was supported by Bill Mayhew, who had joined in 1958 as chief accountant and soon became company secretary.

Bristow bought a house near Cranleigh in Surrey, which became his home for the rest of his working life and on into retirement. With ambitions to move into farming he bought a mixed dairy/arable farm near Reigate, which he renamed Fortune Farm, and later sold it to buy the nearby Baynards Park estate. He also bought a Rolls-Royce, registration plate BHL14 – to represent the fourteen helicopters on the strength at the time. Original directors George Fry, Alan Green and Jack Woolley also benefited from the sale, and were able to set themselves up in the Home Counties around London.

Although Bristow had left Bermuda for good, his companies continued to function there until the late eighties, when the UK tax regulations closed the remaining financial loopholes. Until then, the parent company had an obligation to provide 'management and control' from the island and a stint on Bermuda became a sought-after job for executives. Bill Mayhew, administration directors Philip Warcup and Alan Leahy – to mention just three – each spent several years there fulfilling that role. Mayhew went twice.

The first overhaul to take place in a rented hangar at Redhill was this Bell 47G2 – possibly ex-Bolivia. Bernard Rose is the engineer on the right.

The Airwork company has a long, proud history and was providing aircraft and services to the Royal Air Force before the Second World War. RAF student pilots were quite likely to have trained on Airwork Tiger Moths maintained by Airwork technicians.

However, with the post-war decline in production, the fifties were not an easy time for aviation. Too many companies chased too little business and the government of the day urged rationalisation. In a bid to expand between 1958 and 1959, Airwork acquired several smaller operators – Transair, Aviation Traders, Air Charter and Channel Air Bridge (from Freddie Laker) and finally Morton-Olley Air Services.

Even then there was much duplication of effort so, in 1960, Airwork and Hunting-Clan merged to form British United Airways. With this, the remaining private shareholders in the group relinquished their shares in the parent company and the vice-chairman, Alan Muntz, retired. His place was taken by the chairman of British & Commonwealth Shipping, Sir Nicholas Cayzer. B&C had been the principal partner in Hunting-Clan and was now the largest shareholder in the new group. Bristow came to greatly admire Cayzer as a man of his word while Cayzer had time for any of his businesses that turned a decent profit. By now, BHL was certainly achieving this.

Satisfied with a state of relative economic security, the government introduced legislation to open more opportunities for independents like BUA. The new operator ordered new VC10 and BAC-111 airliners and applied for a considerable number of route licences across the UK and to the Channel Islands, as well as further afield to Africa and the Middle East. In 1961 BUA merged with Silver City Airlines and, later that year, with British Aviation Services.

Finally, a new group known as Air Holdings was born, with both BHL and Airwork as fully-owned subsidiaries. Alan Bristow, George Fry, Jack Woolley and Alan Green – known as the Four Musketeers – subsequently bought back 49% of both companies, resigned as directors of Bristow and formed a new company, Helicopter Contractors, to manage BHL/Airwork interests. This was subsequently renamed Bristow Helicopter Group Ltd.

Some time before this, in 1960, Myles Wyatt had asked Alan Bristow if he would like to take over the running of their sister company Fison-Airwork. This company had evolved from Pest Control Ltd from where, eight years previously, Jack Woolley had arrived. Sir Myles now wanted to merge it with BHL. By the end of the fifties, Fison-Airwork was engaged in spraying crops, particularly banana plantations in the Caribbean and Central America, and oil support. Hiller 12As also sprayed cotton in the Sudan and still more bananas in the British Cameroons.

As early as 1955, Fison-Airwork had become involved in the first oil exploration work in Nigeria, on contract to the Shell D'Arcy development company, which was

Pest Control Hiller 12A, crop spraying cotton in Sudan, 1959.

WS51 Spraying – location unknown.

to evolve into Shell BP. Originally engaged to help in geophysical surveying efforts, the helicopter requirement grew substantially as oil was found in commercial quantities. The Hillers were soon replaced by Whirlwind 1s, as discoveries in Soku introduced the need for men to be transported between a growing number of rigs in the Niger River delta. Fison pilot Bryan Shaw served at Owerri during 1957-1958 and, a year later, as base manager at Port Harcourt. His experience of flying both types would bear significant fruit for BHL, after his return to the UK.

It was at this point that Alan Bristow moved in. A hands–on manager, he set off to visit the various Fison operations around the world. He didn't like what he found. He discovered that the pilots were being asked, in his view, to undertake dangerous missions and that many of them were being paid derisory salaries. This was a little unfair, as many were former fixed-wing pilots who had converted onto helicopters at Fison's expense and who were contracted to pay off the company's investment. This became increasingly common practice and, indeed, BHL later placed similar 'training bonds' on its own student pilots.

Clive Wright in Owerri, Nigeria.

In Nigeria.

Spraying from a WS51.

Widgeon landing on DB2, mangrove swamp, February 1964.

G-AOYB approaching drilling barge No.1 at Ekulama, Rivers Province, Niger Delta, December 1958.

Bristow did not think much of crop-spraying either. From his own experience in France and North Africa he thought it was dangerous and, as it was usually seasonal, not very profitable either. Although helicopters were more efficient, specialist fixed-wing aircraft could carry out the work at a much lower cost per acre. He soon disposed of that part of the business and swiftly put the pilots onto UK commercial pay rates. They of course thought this was wonderful.

However Fison was not an amateur operation. It owned more aircraft and, in Nigeria anyway, had far more experience than BHL. As well as hardware, some extremely able people arrived at the Bristow base: many of whom progressed to senior positions within the company. Unqualified accounts clerk Bryan Collins went on to become managing director and CEO. John Odlin and Bryan Shaw eventually took directorships. Bob Brewster, Peter Gray, John Waddington and Clive Wright became senior pilots and managers. Don Strange, Cliff Saffron and Jim (Mac) Macaskill became senior engineers. Operations director David Bond also joined for a time, before leaving to form his own business.

One Fison engineer, Tommy Bayden, was desperate to fly and eventually made it as a BHL pilot – for a time the only pilot-cum-engineer the company had. Such was the migration that many would later claim that it was Fison that had taken over BHL. Certainly, for a while, Bristow had no shareholding in the company. In fact it was a marriage of just-about-equals.

Clive Wright (left) and 'Mac' Macaskill, Nigeria 1957.

The administrative workload that came with all these mergers was time consuming and, at times, a distraction to BHL's core business. However it was also, now and again, an advantage to be able to introduce the bidder for a contract as Airwork rather than the already better-known BHL. US companies, in particular, were expanding aggressively beyond their shores and, if they thought it necessary, were prepared to dish the dirt on a competitor.

This distraction was removed when, in 1965, Myles Wyatt asked Bristow if he would become joint managing director of BUA, alongside Max Stuart-Shaw. The airline was losing money and dealing with trouble from the labour unions. The chairman thought that a more combative MD would complement Shaw's diplomatic skills. True to character, Bristow rejected the offer and, instead, demanded the post of sole managing director and deputy chairman.

The shareholders eventually agreed to this and, in early December 1967, Bristow took the airline's reins in London for what he later acknowledged was a 'two-year ego trip'. He left BHL in the hands of George Fry as managing director, Jack Woolley and Alan Green. Within two weeks of Bristow's arrival at BUA, pilots' union BALPA terminated its agreement with the airline, fully expecting to negotiate more favourable terms with an inexperienced new boss. To its shock he immediately accepted the decision and started to negotiate contracts with individual pilots.

A strike was threatened but Alan stood his ground. He had won the agreement of the major shareholders to suspend operations if necessary. He called the staff, minus the pilots, to a mass meeting in the hangar – 'If the unions can do it', he said, 'why can't I?' – and talked them around to his position. He then fired all the pilots and told them that, if they wanted to work for BUA again, they would have to sign personal contracts as well.

'Over a hectic weekend I worked on the BHL contracts of employment, added a few of the union requirements, put them together in a new agreement and offered it to the BUA pilots. I gave them seven days to think about it and 212 out of the 235 pilots signed up for the deal.'

As a final humiliation of BALPA, Alan talked its secretary general, Philip Warcup, into defecting. Former RAF Air Commodore Warcup had had a distinguished flying career including, during the Malayan emergency, a spell in helicopters. Bristow was scathing during their first meeting. 'You're on the wrong side of the table Warcup! You ought to come and work for me, instead of wasting your time with this lot.'

Two weeks later they met again – this time for a job interview. Alan had one more go at him, for trying to bring down a private enterprise with union muscle, before offering him the job of BUA personnel director. Philip Warcup went on to serve as administration director for BHL throughout the 1970s. However, Bristow's combative stance with the union was to set the scene for a later, far more damaging industrial action against the helicopter company.

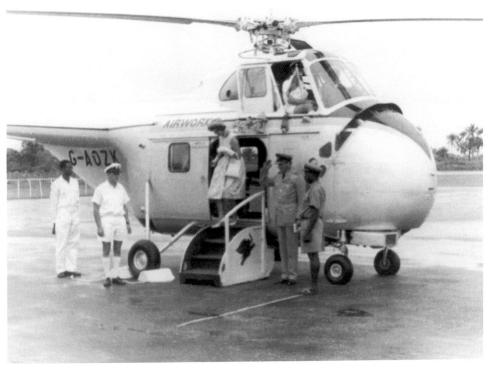

HRH Princess Alexandra arrives in Nigeria. Bryan Shaw is the pilot.

Pierco Airport,
Trinidad, June 1960.

While Bristow was preoccupied at BUA his company, under the stewardship of George Fry, continued to grow. By early 1968, BHL owned over eighty helicopters and employed over 100 pilots: most of them working in support of the oil industry.

Tony Stafford's first BHL posting was to Trinidad. 'We set up a small hangar on the east coast, at Mayaro, with a WS55 and a Bell 206A. Marcel Avon was chief pilot and we initially worked for Pan American Oil with the *Bluewater* 3 rig. In January 1970, we opened a new heliport at Sea Lots, in Port of Spain, and with a second rig coming on site, took on a second Whirlwind.' Trinidad is still a flourishing operation and, indeed, has great promise for the near future.

As well as Trinidad, BHL oil and gas operations flourished in Nigeria and the Persian Gulf. It found work with Esso in Morocco, to where John Whale ferried a Hiller 12E from the UK. It became established off Mauritania, for Woodside Petroleum, and on the north-west shelf of Australia, originally for Burmah Oil. Clive Wright took charge of a contract training pilots for the Kuwait Army on the

Whirlwind. The company was also eyeing the possibilities for oil off Malaysia and Indonesia.

A new contract in Egypt needed some careful handling, particularly in 1967, in the aftermath of the Six-Day War with Israel. Bristow was hoping to support an oil-rig off Ras Shakhir with a couple of Jet Rangers. The day after the ceasefire, George Fry flew out to Cairo to negotiate the contract. He recalls:

*I was concerned during the flight out. Because of its support for Israel, Britain wasn't at all popular in Egypt. However the people were as welcoming as ever. I drove to Shepherd's Hotel to see the customer and the meeting escalated into a party – I remember halfway through someone put a thunderflash in the piano. At some point the manager and I retired to a corner with a bottle of Scotch and, by sunrise, we had negotiated an order for two much bigger Whirlwinds.*

BHL was also starting to make headway in the North Sea. In November 1964 Alan Bristow acted once more as chief salesman and negotiator to secure two small offshore gas contracts, off Eelde in The Netherlands and Emden in Germany. The latter was to service the *Mr Louie* exploration rig, operated by a consortium of oil

Doug Batten with his Hiller 12E aboard the Vinagaroon rig, Trinidad.

companies led by Preusag. Chief pilot Alistair Gordon was supported by Willie Weitzel, John Waddington, Horst Neu and Dick Jones – known as the 'fluid druid'. The Eelde operation was led by John Griffiths.

Willie Weitzel once had an engine failure, close to the rig in his Whirlwind. He carried out a perfect engine-off landing on the sea, from where it was subsequently recovered. BHL crews later flew from Esbjerg in Denmark, for Gulf Oil, and from Haarlingen in The Netherlands. They competed with Okanagan, which was in partnership with BEA Helicopters and operating out of Beccles.

> *In those days* [explains Bryan Collins] *before the strictly controlled bidding procedures we're familiar with today, you became aware of a business opportunity on the horizon and you offered your services to the customer, hopefully ahead of everyone else. We became well-known for keeping our ears to the ground and tapping into oil-industry intelligence. Alan was particularly good at this. I would often hand deliver our proposals, which were detailed enough to be the basis for contracts. I remember talking to Shell in Houston and our contact said how helpful he found them. Whether we got the business or not, it was invaluable customer contact.*

Winning a contract was one thing but getting permission to operate in the country involved was quite another. Local operators would often be outraged that they had missed out on the work and, through better government relationships, could put up any number of obstacles to the work starting. Partnerships were a regular, but not infallible, way around these obstacles.

By the mid-1960s, with operations stretching across the world, confidence at Redhill was rampant. The company had now grown to the point that it could, in the right circumstances, order aircraft 'on spec'. Attracted by a particularly good finance deal – $70,000 each, according to Bryan Collins – it signed up for no fewer than fifteen of the latest Agusta Bell 206 Jet Rangers. 'We didn't have any actual work for them to do: just the thought that they would be useful introductions to the new light gas turbine technology. However we were confident we would find the business.' They soon did, in Australia, Indonesia, Iran and Nigeria, so the deal was worthwhile.

Jack Woolley's engineering department was by now doing much more than maintaining this growing fleet. It was upgrading Hillers and carrying out turbine conversions to its Whirlwinds, substituting the old Pratt & Whitney R1340 air-cooled radials with Rolls-Royce Gnome H1000s – the standard for UK helicopter turbines for many years. The new Series 3 helicopters became known as 'long-nose' Whirlwinds and John Odlin, for one, is convinced that Alan Bristow's decision to employ them, rather than the new single turbine-engined Sikorsky S62, is what gave BHL a strong competitive edge in the international marketplace. 'It gave us a real cost-advantage over operators with the expensive new helicopter, and I have a gut-feeling that that's what helped us take off.'

Bristow was also continually searching for other opportunities to expand and it soon became clear that those earlier contracts off the coasts of north-western Europe represented just the tip of the iceberg. It was time to look further north.

CHAPTER FIVE

# BACK TO THE COLD

On 17 February 1965 one of the new long-nose Whirlwinds (G-APWN) took off from Sunderland's Usworth airfield. It was flown by a new recruit, Bob Roffe, who was being checked out by Alan Green. The helicopter, now consigned to a museum at Coventry Airport, flew to Amoseas' *Mr Cap*, a three-legged jack-up drilling rig 145 miles out on the Dogger Bank.

Bob remembers that, 'with max fuel the payload was 680lbs and Alan Green had promised Amoseas a minimum of four passengers. The problem was that our boys were burly lads who all weighed over 200lbs – one, a toolpusher by the name of Bill Kilgore, came in at 280lbs. Getting him into the immersion suit was a three man effort. Thank goodness for lots of wind.'

The flight took two hours and fifteen minutes and was monitored, via a plot back at base, by Jack Brannon. After dropping one group of passengers and picking up another, Roffe made the return journey to Usworth. It was the first of several million Bristow Helicopters revenue sectors to be flown over the North Sea.

Further south, Clive Wright was chief pilot of two caravans at North Denes airfield, near Great Yarmouth, and a second Whirlwind (G-APDY). An ex-Air Whaling and Fison pilot, and an old hand at remote operations, Wright made his first sortie on 23 April 1965; flying DY to the Glomar IV exploration rig, thirty to forty miles off the coast. Over the next three or four years the number of rigs in the southern sector would increase from one or two to over twenty. The number of helicopters and crews required to service them would have to grow accordingly.

Six months earlier, the British government had announced the award of offshore concessions on the UK-controlled area of the continental shelf. Of the original eleven tenders that were put out, asking for bids to operate helicopter services, BHL won ten. The announcement precipitated a party of historic proportions at Redhill where, during one of several pranks, Alan Green distributed a crate of North Sea herring. In the event they ended up being flung around with wild abandon by Bristow employees, decked out in full oilskins.

G-APWN at *Mr Cap*, February 1965.

WN, now put out to grass at Coventry.

On approach to *Mr Cap*.

Admittedly, BHL had a head start. Its emergence as a real force in the commercial operating field could be traced back to those early days in the Persian Gulf. With operations in Germany and The Netherlands, it had also gained experience in flying over the North Sea. However, the winning of the bulk of these tenders was no formality and, despite BHL's experience and reputation, it had to sell itself very hard. Both the major British operators, and many of the minor ones, were pitching aggressively to gain a piece of what they all sensed could be something big.

BHL was taking a huge gamble in the future of the oil industry in the North Sea. For one thing, its experience to date had been gained almost exclusively overseas – the Middle East, South America, West Africa and the Caribbean – where the climates were benign in comparison to what they would have to face 'up there'. Equally, its offshore experience had been confined to rigs which lay relatively close to shore. Here they would be making 150-200 mile transits on a daily basis. This would involve the extensive use of modern, twin-engined helicopters.

Even so, had those been the only problems that BHL's participation had to overcome, then the exercise would have amounted only to a calculated risk. But there was more at stake. The contracts with the oil companies required the exclusive use of one or more helicopters and were renewable every one or two years. Only if these renewals went ahead, would BHL stand to recoup its initial investment in the helicopters and achieve reasonable profits. In the event, renewals became all but automatic and, for a decade, oil companies even became associated with individual operators.

When these initial contracts were being negotiated, it was impossible to tell if there was oil and gas in sufficient quantities to justify the companies staying there. By mid-1967, BHL's total investment in the project stood at £2.5 million and it had budgeted to recover its outlay over five years. The decision to bid for these contracts was not as obvious as it may now seem.

The company set about establishing its North Sea presence with military precision. One critical bridge to build was that of its relationship with the Ministry of Aviation (now the Civil Aviation Authority). Although at the time the Ministry retained no in-house helicopter expertise, it would keep a keen eye on activity in the British sector. Discussions centred around two vital issues: weather minima and the level of equipment carried in the helicopters.

Alan Bristow was adamant that two engines were the basic requirement, and soon introduced the fourteen-passenger-seat Wessex 60 – another Sikorsky airframe built under licence by Westland, powered by two Rolls-Royce Gnome turbines. The S61N, later to become a mainstay of all North Sea operations, was viewed at the time by the company as 'hellishly expensive'. In the event the Ministry accepted the BHL proposals and the resultant standards and procedures became accepted practice across the North Sea.

When the first concession awards were announced, it was not known where the majority of the oil companies planned to start drilling. The areas under discussion extended from north of the Shetlands to just north of the Thames Estuary and it was obvious from the start that many of the initial operations would have to be carried out from temporary bases. The first of these were in the southern sector of the North Sea. Sunderland to the north, in February 1965, was followed by North Denes in the south. Then came Tetney and, by March 1966, Grimsby and Scarborough.

Tetney operations to the BP West Sole gas field continued until 1968, after which a smaller service operated from the small grass airfield of Paull, on the Humber Estuary. However, North Denes was by far the biggest operation and, within a year, Clive Wright's caravans had been replaced by a permanent heliport, handling a

Wessex 60 undergoing offshore maintenance.

Wessex 60 at North Denes, 1969.

This WS55-1 supported offshore oil and gas exploration in the Irish Sea, from a base at Blackpool, June 1969.

Wessex 60 and five Whirlwinds. More Wessex arrived and an instrument flying training school was set up to service the expanding sector.

In November 1968 the *Hewitt Alpha* rig blew out. Five Wessex were scrambled from North Denes and succeeded in recovering the twenty-nine survivors. However, while rushing to its aid, supply ship *Hector Gannet* capsized and three members of her crew died. BHL pilots out of North Denes winched survivors up from the local lifeboat and flew them back to base, from where they were transferred to hospital.

Two years later a platform under tow, the *Constellation*, broke loose and sank, but not before all twenty-two men on board had been rescued by a Bristow helicopter.

One day during lunch aboard *Mr Cap*, Bob Roffe was asked by the outgoing drilling crew if he could make a fly-by, door-side to the rig, so that they could take photographs.

*I circled at low level and was surprised to see a fusillade of oranges being hurled out of the aircraft towards the drilling deck. I put this down to crew-change exuberance. An hour into the flight I also found out, from the passenger in the co-pilot's seat, that one of the cabin passengers had reached up and tied his bootlaces together, over and around the stub base for the co-pilot's cyclic – the stick had been removed for single pilot operation.*

*After checking that I still had full control, I called North Denes on HF and asked them to get Global Marine's drilling manager Jack Pillow, to meet me on arrival. The good Texan was busy and wanted to know more, but quickly agreed when I told him my next call would be to the police. The aircraft landed, the evidence exposed and the guilty parties banned by me from crew-changing by air. After two boat changes in rough weather, Jack and I agreed that normal service could be resumed. I later learned that bottles of whisky had come out to the rig in my helicopter, for them to enjoy on the flight home!*

Clive Wright flies a WS60 to the *Orion* rig.

New blades for a Wessex 60 at North Denes.

Wessex at North Denes. (Photo *Financial Times*)

*Opposite* North Denes Wessex helping to construct the base of Royal Sovereign Light Tower, off Beachy Head. (Photo Malcolm Pendrill)

On a PNR (point of no return) operation the reliability of rig weather assumes some importance, especially as the Dogger Bank is renowned for generating fog. BHL rules defined rig minimum visibility as half a mile for the Decca ADF navaids, which sounded fine, until you realised that one centimetre on the Decca flight log map equated to ten nautical miles at the rig site. Bob Roffe again:

*I should have known it was radio operator Albert's crew change day, one nice April morning at Usworth, when Jack received the rig weather as light winds in a stable 'high'. 'No cloud, hazy, vis one mile.' At PNR the minimum rig vis was three-quarters of a mile. Ten miles further on it was half a mile decreasing and, ten miles from the rig, we were in thick fog. By that time I was at 40 feet and winding the (HF) aerial in!*

*We crabbed in, with the ASI just indicating and the ADF needle 30 degrees to starboard, and the passenger in the co-pilot's seat briefed to shout if he saw anything. The accursed Albert had been ordered to stick his head out of his deck radio shack and yell when he heard us. To cut a long, sphincter-puckering 30 minute story short, with the ADF ident very noisy, the Decca map needle on the rig, Albert shouting 'I hear you' and the passenger assuming as much of a foetal position as he could, the rig leg appeared out of the fog. It required some nifty control inputs to pull up and, without losing visual contact, fast-stop over the deck. When Albert came out of hiding to admit his sins, and had been thoroughly 'picturised' by me, I took him back with the rest of his crew. We flew over solid fog, surface to 3,000 feet, all the way back.*

Wessex 60 with Shell tanker.

Other aircrew who flew Wessex out of North Denes included Michel Thomas, Gordon Lucas, Peter Donaldson, Ben Breech and John Whale. They ran a strict schedule: four passenger flights out from the terminal every morning, shut down on one of the rigs – referred to, somewhat prosaically, by numbers such as *18A* or *27B* – and the same back in the evening. At the time there were about twenty rigs in total: by 2002 the number would grow to well over 100.

By 1967, it was becoming obvious that the gamble of two years earlier was beginning to pay off. Both exploration and exploitation off the coast was there to stay and BHL was putting more and more of its effort into servicing that industry. Some 80% of its 25,000 hours of revenue flying could be accounted for by offshore work. And there was talk of an even richer bonanza off the Scottish coast.

There was no sudden spurt of activity to the north, however. A Whirlwind in the hands of Ernie Perrin flew from Aberdeen for the first time in July 1967. During the

*Opposite:* BHL took on *ad hoc* charters as well. Here a Wessex 60 lifts a generator for a London rooftop. (Photo Mirror Newspapers)

Alan Green (left) with Alan Bristow at Battersea Heliport, preparing to take delivery of the first Wessex 60 – BHL's 100th helicopter.

North Denes expansion.

New offices at Redhill were built to Jack Woolley's specification. (Photo Malcolm Pendrill)

summer of 1969, a Wessex 60 was sent there to fly on a contract for BP. In August 1971 a handful of pilots and support staff moved into the Second World War-vintage accommodation which then lined Aberdeen Airport's western perimeter, with a twenty-four-seat Sikorsky S61N, a second-hand machine fresh from a failed public transport operation in Italy. Engineers including John Wilson hated working on that aircraft because the engine filters were all in the 'wrong' place.

A second S61N from the same source, which had been involved in a heavy landing, was rebuilt to flying status at Redhill and delivered the following February – after a little local difficulty in getting it out of the hangar. It was too tall to be towed out and trenches had to be dug in the hangar floor and a hole cut in the roof. Not long after this, plans were put in place to build bigger hangars and offices at Redhill.

BHL wasn't the first operator to arrive in Aberdeen. BEA Helicopters had been there from earlier in 1967 and its own chief executive, 'Jock' Cameron, widely regarded as a visionary equal to Alan Bristow, was the first to operate the S61N. This helicopter had a 'stand-up' cabin and quickly proved popular with passengers. Cameron's company was also backed by public money; enabling it to undercut BHL on some of the early contract bids.

The real Aberdeen expansion began around 1970, after Alan Bristow had returned from running BUA. Bill Petrie recalled the start of the build-up well. 'It was clear that Dyce Airport was going to be the main hub so we meant to be there. We had

Alan Bristow at North Denes.

Aberdeen, 1970s. (Photo Malcolm Pendrill)

to make a fairly dramatic upgrade to the Aberdeen management – to start with there was only a chief pilot and engineer – so John Odlin, engineer Jim Macaskill and I went to supervise the expansion.'

The company had also made the decision to invest in more S61Ns. 'We built a hangar for a couple of them; then a passenger terminal and then more hangars and workshops. We approved the designs on the latter project and had actually started work – the foundations were laid and the steel about to be erected – when we decided to turn everything through 90 degrees and build it twice as big. We doubled the size of the terminal as well'. The project took several years to complete: in the meantime a lot of time was spent working out of Portakabins.

A problem that both BHL and BEAH faced was that pilots were at a premium. The Cold War was at its height and the supply of ex-military crews had slowed to a trickle. At one stage, in May 1971, flying training superintendent Mike Norris was sent over to New York to recruit ex-service American pilots for overseas BHL operations. He flight-tested twenty of them over a three-day period. A Redhill training school grew to accommodate three courses a year, each of six *ab initio* students, that helped to ease the strain.

The decision to establish such a major and costly presence at Aberdeen paid off, as the activities of the oil companies in the northern sector of the North Sea continued to grow apace. During the fifteen years following that first flight in February 1965, the North Sea accounted for a sixth of all the flying hours and a third of all the passengers flown by BHL around the world. In 1980 alone nearly 400,000 passengers and over 2,300 tonnes of freight passed through the BHL terminal: throughput that threatened to overwhelm the already stretched operation.

In the summer of 1972, BHL sent a single S61N to share a war-time hangar with BEA Helicopters at Sumburgh, in South Shetland, on a three-day-week contract for Shell's *Bluewater III* and *Glomar V* rigs. Oil workers flew there from Aberdeen by fixed-wing, on the premise that the further you could get without using the more expensive helicopters, the better.

Bill Petrie again:

> The main management difficulty we faced at Sumburgh was one of persuading people to actually go there. There was no accommodation so we had to build eight bungalows at Hardbrakes, a few miles north of the airfield. These were occupied on a 'hot bunk' basis by rotating crews. When in time families followed them, further staff housing was built.
>
> The families issue gave us quite a headache. In the winter it doesn't get light until 9.30 a.m. and it's dark again by 3.30 p.m. Many families found it difficult to cope with such long periods of darkness. In the summer it hardly gets dark – which can be just as bad. Try telling the kids to go to bed when it's still broad daylight.

The number of offshore support helicopters at Sumburgh grew substantially during the 1970s with, at its peak, thirty S61N daily flights from the small airport. These were supported by a twenty-four-hour maintenance operation. The activity expanded to the stage where fixed-wing aircraft, having brought the oil workers to

S61N
underslinging
flare-stack
components.

the airport, had to position to Kirkwall in Orkney for the day. It was a rare example of helicopters taking priority over aeroplanes.

Operating problems were, in the main, created by the harsh environment, but the expansion itself had to be handled carefully. The financial skills of Alan Bristow played a part in this.

> At one stage, during a period where the rate of expansion threatened our cash flow, I managed to persuade the oil companies to accept 'front-end loaded' contracts, a principle which was later extended to some Aberdeen contracts. These gave us a high recovery rate for one or two years and then, when the rates dropped off, we got our cash-flow back in balance. Then our clients had the option of extending the contract at a lower rate.
>
> I'm glad we did that. The period didn't last very long but it was long enough to get us over a hump – a very important hump.

Bryan Collins acknowledges that the cash flow was 'brilliant'.

Bill Petrie recalls that they could not build hangars quickly enough to keep up with the numbers of helicopters arriving, 'so we always had a problem with aircraft parked out in the open. The wind blows across the islands like no other place on earth, so we had to find ways of securing the rotor blades. Alan's experiences in the Antarctic gave us a lead here. Our blade supports worked very well and, on several occasions, we'd have aircraft parked outside and diverted Royal Navy Sea Kings would park alongside for the night. We'd come out in the morning after a stormy night, take off our supports, start up and away we'd go. The Navy, on the other hand, would be left looking gloomily at their damaged blades and would have to sit around, sometimes for days, waiting for spares'.

As the oil companies became aware of their versatility, the helicopters took on an increasing number of roles. However, as far as the roughnecks were concerned, one function superseded all others. As with that *Mr Cap* crew, they knew the helicopters were their ticket home. They coveted the facility and, if there was any uncertainty that they would be relieved, had no compunction in bending the rules. Incidents similar to the one experienced by Bob Roffe on the Dogger Bank, became a feature of early operations.

Snow and ice didn't bother the civil S61Ns.

George Fry in a Wessex 60.

One North Sea veteran recalls:

*Platforms are relatively stable but, early on, we operated a fair bit off ships – small vessels like the Cappalonga and the Samarkand. Cappalonga was a converted tanker with a helipad on its superstructure and the swell could generate a hell of a lot of pitch and roll. Now there are strict regulations about the limits, concerning whether a helicopter could land or not, but come the day of the crew change, whatever state the sea was actually in, the Cappalonga was always within limits. If you radio'd down to ask what their pitch and roll was, they'd reply that it was 'two and two'. You could see perfectly well that it must be more like seven or eight, but you still had to go and land on the bloody thing.*

Operations like that emphasised the importance of teamwork and the need for pilot and co-pilot to work in conjunction, to assess a situation and undertake the calculated risk:

*In those early days it was a purely personal judgement – what you thought you and your crew were capable of – and a bit of luck. But it was always a team effort. If your co-pilot was on his knees because he'd flown a lot of hours that day, then you might think twice about it, especially if it was a night flight. Even if it's just a case of bad weather, you can cope rather better if he just takes the radio chat away from you. It's rather different now because roles are far more clearly defined, but in those days it was ultimately your responsibility. The calls came directly to you and you made the decision.*

When BHL had won the first North Sea contracts with the Wessex 60, it also won a short-term battle with BEAH. However it fell behind in the fight to provide customers with all-weather capability, which quickly became a 'must have' for North Sea operations.

To offer an all-but-guaranteed service a helicopter requires not only two engines, but also full flight instrumentation and an autopilot – the ability for the pilot to fly 'hands-off' and rely on his instruments during the approach. The BEAH Sikorsky S61N was better fitted for instrument flying than was the BHL Wessex. Alastair Gordon was instrumental in developing, with Ferranti, an autopilot to add that capability to the older type. On 29 May 1970, Bob Roffe and Bob Balls made BHL's first revenue IFR offshore flight from North Denes in a Wessex.

The first Bell 212, a twin-engined fifteen-seater with great utility potential, was certificated in mid-1971 and initially deployed overseas. It also had teething problems – its stability augmentation system was not authorised for flying hands-off below 40 knots – but eventually earned its spurs as an invaluable workhorse in BHL operations. In particular, its two-blade configuration proved extremely useful when it came to protecting them in the narrow hangars on rigs and platforms.

Sikorsky production line, 1973.

Significantly, British Executive Air Services (BEAS) was the first to operate the type over the North Sea in 1975. BHL would continue the routine after its purchase of BEAS, two years later.

The potential for offshore business continued to build and BHL, intent on competing with the state-financed BEAH, decided to 'go for broke' with an order for no fewer than twenty-six new S61s, essentially the rest of the production schedule on Sikorsky's Connecticut line. The first ex-factory machines (in order G-BAKB, KA and KC) arrived in March 1973 and thereafter, recalls Mike Norris, 'they seemed to be turning up every second month'. The influx was such that Mike became fully involved in training the pilots and had to insist on flying the line now and again, in order to remain current with offshore flying techniques.

In those days, new pilots were given a great deal of responsibility. When John Whale was appointed to Aberdeen as a captain in 1973, he had a grand total of eight hours – the length of his conversion – on the S61N. His first flight was to a rig named *Pacesetter 2* and he was told, almost in passing, 'Oh by the way John, the autopilot doesn't work'. He set off with nineteen passengers on a Decca track which, although a straight line in reality, on the map in front of him described a graceful parabola. 'Not good for pilot confidence.'

Like most experienced pilots, John is horrified at the thought of some of the things he did in the early days. 'We felt an obligation to get the job done, whatever the conditions. Although we weren't put under pressure, we knew that the company wouldn't get paid if the job wasn't completed. It was a matter of pride. Now the regulations are such that we fly to their limits and no further. You know exactly where you stand, and that has to be a better way of working.'

Early landing pads were delineated only with painted circles, often designed for single-engined helicopters such as the Jet Ranger, so the handling pilot in the much larger S61N had to judge his landing carefully. The pads themselves were usually the last bit to have been tacked on during construction, with no thought given to obstructions or the position of the turbine exhausts. The Forties platforms, in particular, had a bad reputation for deck turbulence.

A smaller than expected helideck, coupled with some awkward deck movement, contributed to the loss of G-AZNE, the 'original' UK S61N, in 1973. While landing on the drillship *Glomar North Sea*, eighty to a hundred miles to the east of Aberdeen, the handling pilot touched down too far aft, allowing his tail wheel to drop into the safety netting around the helideck. At the other end the nose tipped sharply up. The pilot instinctively tried to correct it with forward cyclic and the rotor disc came down sharply, chopping off the top of the cockpit and the overhead console. The engine speed select levers went too, so the mercifully unharmed pilots could no longer shut down.

The master of the vessel, concerned for its safety, ordered the pilot to take off. Having disembarked his co-pilot and passengers he tried to do just that, but overpitched and ended up ditching in a heavy swell. He quickly extricated himself; leaving the unfortunate helicopter to meander around in circles until its fuel ran out. This process took four and a half hours. When the rotors finally stopped, an attempt was made to recover the S61N to the deck of a nearby supply vessel. Unfortunately the airframe broke in two and sank. A solitary sponson was washed up on a Danish beach many months later.

Following this incident, UK operators sat down with the Civil Aviation Authority (CAA) to develop criteria for landing on UK offshore structures. Current regulations can be traced back to these meetings in 1973.

Although the S61N quickly became popular with both passengers, who liked the roomy cabin, and crews who loved its reliability, it was not the perfect answer. Even after Alastair Gordon succeeded in increasing its all-up weight, the single-engine performance of the S61N was never going to be wonderful. Alan Bristow said at the time that Westland made a 'major error' in declining his order for ten civil-certificated Sea Kings, which had better performance and greater range. Sikorsky's new S70, a civil variant of the military Black Hawk, seemed to have a bright future so space on the production line had to be made available. As it turned out, while Black Hawk variants went on to dominate the military utility market, the S70 took an age to become certified and the delay led to BHL cancelling an order for ten of them.

Aberdeen expanded with the arrival of S61Ns.

By 1975 Bristow was operating from Aberdeen and Sumburgh with eighteen S61Ns, a Wessex 60 and a Jet Ranger. Together with BEAH, it had also acquired ten ex-military piston-engined Sikorsky S58s, which BHL converted to run with Pratt & Whitney PT6-6 gas turbines (Chapter 12). The company was also providing the bulk of the profits within its parent group. Each of the helicopters was averaging 100 hours a month, flying anywhere from the East Shetland Basin to the Danish coast.

A regular S61N flight from Aberdeen to the Forties oilfield would involve a take-off and departure to the north-east at one of three altitudes, with positions being fixed on the Decca Mk19 moving map and passed to the company every ten to fifteen minutes. A missed call would trigger an immediate alert. Flight watch was provided by the company. A common frequency enabled traffic to keep a mental note of possible conflicts, and was shared with RAF patrol aircraft in the area.

Because most of the rigs and platforms were below its radar horizon, Buchan Radar on the mainland could provide only a listening watch. The crew would make radio contact with the structures on their route as soon as possible, to confirm passenger numbers and work out their most economical route between them. As the helicopter approached, its own radar, switched to ground-mapping mode, would pick up the correct platform and, hopefully, its not very reliable non-directional beacon (NDB). Letting down to minimum height above the sea (150ft), the co-pilot would look out until he made visual contact and then set up a visual approach to the helideck. Procedures were developed to make offset approaches, which left the rig to appear on the handling pilot's side of the aircraft. Once on the platform, either the helicopter or the rig itself would announce its safe arrival to Dyce.

When relatively few helicopters were flying, separation wasn't really an issue and the height was dictated by the weather and the captain's background. Ex-Navy fliers tended to fly relatively close to the sea and Army and Air Force pilots stayed as far away from the stuff as possible. Safety equipment consisted of a life jacket. However, as activity grew exponentially during the 1970s, to achieve correct flight separation a system of outbound and inbound altitudes and radials was introduced. Floatable padded 'Musk-ox' jackets were superseded by today's familiar survival suits and life rafts made an appearance for the first time.

The January 1974 rescue of 150 crewmembers from the *Trans Ocean III* and *Trans World 62* rigs is described in Chapter 11. However, the incident brought the issue of providing survival equipment for everyone flying over the North Sea into sharp focus.

## CHAPTER SIX

# ALL RIGHT VILLAGE?

Each of the British armed forces has an air wing and its traditions, duties and roles are fiercely protected. The Army Air Corps' (AAC) birth in 1957 was a painful delivery by anybody's standards and inter-service rivalry led, in its early days, to severely restricted levels of government funding. In particular, the new Corps suffered from a shortage of aircraft and very sparse facilities.

Bryan Shaw left the Army, as a captain, in the same year as the Corps' foundation and soon found work with Fison Airwork on the Shell D'Arcy contract in Nigeria. He then spent a year working in Pakistan on an oil contract in the North-west Frontier province, before returning to the UK. During his leave he made contact with some of his former Army colleagues, who all suggested it might be worth making a bid to the Army to 'civilianise' some or all of its flying training. They cited its lack of funding and the consequent fact that the aircraft and crews required for the task, had to come from the same pool of men as that of the operational squadrons.

Over the next three years Shaw, during visits to the Redhill office, suggested that this idea should be investigated. It was clear that the shortages were already adversely affecting the AAC's training and front-line capability.

*Using civilians would have the effect of releasing service aircraft and personnel for operational duties. The civil instructors would provide continuity and they would also want to be there, whereas any army pilots who stayed at the AAC's headquarters at Middle Wallop (MW) beyond their original tour, risked damaging their career prospects. The army would tell us what they wanted in terms of syllabus, while we would provide the helicopters and military-trained and approved instructors. They would be able to judge how it worked over a three year contract.*

In 1961, at the height of both the Cold War and the Aden and Borneo emergencies, an unexpected opportunity arose to demonstrate how this might be done. The Royal Navy had converted one of its aircraft carriers, HMS *Bulwark*, into a commando carrier and the concept of landing marines by helicopter suited the amphibious concept then

Bryan Shaw in Pakistan.

Toasting the success of the RN training are, left to right: Bryan Shaw, Alastair Gordon, a student, chief engineer Ted Greenwell, a secretary, SNO Lt-Cdr Peter Chinn and George Fry.

being championed by the First Sea Lord, Lord Mountbatten. He soon decided to commission a second, HMS *Albion*, which would be supported by Whirlwind Mk1s from 846 Naval Air Squadron. These helicopters needed crews and, because the Navy's own training programme was saturated, a tender invitation went out to civil companies, inviting them to bid for a contract to train naval personnel on the Whirlwinds. The Mk1 was equivalent to a Series 1 – a type not unfamiliar to BHL.

With the experience gained in training pilots in Kuwait, BHL won the Navy contract in 1961 and set up a training school at its Redhill headquarters. It offered basic training on Hiller 12Bs and Cs, many of which had to be refurbished after being in storage after earlier whaling and spraying contracts, and conversion courses to the Whirlwind. The ex-military instructors went through a Central Flying School syllabus, were standardised by a visiting 'trappers' team and then trained four courses, comprising in total thirty-two officers. Only two of them failed to make the grade and were 'chopped'.

The students, all qualified officers with at least one sea-going appointment under their belts, had a whale of a time at Redhill. They were billeted in a nearby country

The first Royal Navy course at Redhill. (Fox Photos)

One of four RN courses that passed through Redhill. Peter Voute is first left at rear and John Willis, who later joined BHL, is next to him.

club and the senior officer on the course qualified for a double bed. The club was also used by Scandinavian Air Services' crews passing through London Gatwick. Sub-Lt Peter Voute remembers that the training was professional, with no problems re-adapting to service flying afterwards, but also that the social life took on legendary proportions.

Peter went on to become a Captain RN, but still remembers his first Whirlwind night solo.

> We carried flares that, in case of an engine failure, we could set off to illuminate the ground. They did have a habit of igniting spontaneously, however. As I turned crosswind there was a bright flash to my port side so, in the belief that I had a phosphorus flare burning next to my fuselage, I put out a Mayday and auto-rotated down to the field. Surrounded by fire-wagons I climbed out, to find all the flares still in place. I had been taken in by a flash from an electric train, passing a pylon underneath. I was not popular.
>
> During the previous course, while they were on the Hiller stage, one student decided to find out how many 360 degree turns he could do in autorotation from 1,000ft. Half way round his third, he ploughed into the airfield. He was collected from the wreckage by Alan Bristow himself and taken to his office, where he was plied with whisky until the assurance assessor arrived!

Hiller 12Bs, Middle Wallop, November 1964.

Peter's opinion is that the stop-gap training system worked well. Both squadrons earned a high reputation in operations in the jungles of Borneo, in support of the Army and Marines, from 1962-1964.

When the director of land/air warfare, General Pat Weston, decided that the AAC would outsource its training on a trial basis – 'I have no doubt that the RAF advised against it', says Bryan Shaw – BEA Helicopters and Bristow were the main contenders. To be accurate Airwork, a wholly-owned subsidiary of Air Holdings which was obliged to sign any government contract, was the bidder. When it won, it arranged to sub-contract the helicopter work, the major part of the deal, to BHL. Airwork instructors took on the initial 'flying grading', first on Army-owned Austers, then de Havilland Chipmunks, also at Middle Wallop. Over the ensuing years, the distinction between the two companies all but disappeared.

The service began at MW on 1 April 1963, just before BHL's tenth birthday. It has run, with renewals and re-bids, for forty years. Bryan Shaw was brought back from Trinidad, where he was serving as chief pilot, to manage the ex-Air Force and Navy instructors who were recruited. Shaw and most of his team set up home in the area, buying property in the confidence that the three-year contract would be extended.

They were proved right and the contract quickly grew to be a significant Bristow profit centre. BHL also supplied the maintenance and, by 1968, air traffic control and ground school instruction – the Airwork and BHL roles also swapped in this year, with the latter becoming lead contractor.

Twenty-two Hillers A, B and C's were brought in from spraying contracts all over the world. BHL engineers converted the overhead-cyclic As into Bs and fitted military PTR170, 12-crystal UHF sets to them all. They shared a packed Hangar Three with over thirty Chipmunks, of which the vast majority would fly every day. When full, it was much quicker to walk round the outside of the hangar than try and get across it. One of the Chipmunks used for glider towing at nearby Netheravon sported camouflage colours – and became known as the 'Spitmunk'.

*Some of the older Army types were unhappy with the Hiller as a basic trainer, [says Shaw]. They argued that it was hard to fly. I had to fight our corner on this point on a number of occasions, arguing that while the reverse throttle reaction – experienced during the early stages of lifting the collective – required good co-ordination from a student, in the long run the practice made for better pilots. I also pointed out that the US Navy and Army had both successfully used the 12A, B and C, before progressing to the E.*

*Before the days of towing frames [says A&E fitter Steve Cooper] we had to use ropes to pull the Hillers, with handling wheels fitted to the skids, out of the hangar.*
*There's quite a slope just outside and you needed to judge your pull quite finely, especially if you wanted to make the dispersal without running into the grass.*
*When the heavier Bell 47s arrived we were given an electric handling trolley, a bit like a stripped-down milk float. We fitted a pilot's cyclic to it, with all the switches wired up, so that one man could do the whole job by himself. It's wrecked now but I remember it running around the perimeter track. It could get up quite a speed with a battery booster pack. If the greenies drove it down to Hangar 4, the army pilots would often ask if they could take it for a spin.*

Ready for the day. B47G4As.

The Spitmunk.

BHL support to the AAC extended to providing additional air traffic services at Netheravon, assistance in seventy REME (Royal Electrical and Mechanical Engineers) workshops and maintenance of operational helicopters being rotated from Northern Ireland duties. At its peak, over 200 employees were committed to the contract.

Ted Greenwell was a formidable chief engineer during the early days, who later ran the WS55 Gnome engine conversions at Redhill. His ground staff were almost all Hampshire natives, who would invariably greet each other with 'all right village?' At the time they joined the company, many of them were complete strangers to aviation. Avionics engineer Frank Dench was a TV engineer and bowser driver Curly Day a turkey plucker. They needed training and much of this was done in-house, but some were sent to Redhill for courses.

*It was always a hive of activity* [remembers Frank] *and, especially in the early days, we regularly put in seven-day weeks. We soon worked out that, if we were required to get all 16 Hillers out on the line by 0800, we needed to 'turn-to' 20 minutes before the laid-down time of 0750. Once they were all airborne we had a chance to relax, and often start a sweepstake to bet which student would be first to knock his tail boom off after an autorotation.*

Reg Barnes was a senior A&C engineer at MW, and, after he had been trained to hover and avoid ground resonance, became the only engineer cleared to ground run

The Bristow team at Middle Wallop, Summer 1970.

Bell 47. (Photo Malcolm Pendrill)

Eddie Ford (left) and David Mallock (right) congratulate instructor Ray Elliott on passing 10,000 hours.

the Hillers. His son Peter was trained by the company as a pilot and rose to become head of flight operations.

In the early days of the contract, when the Corps was still in its infancy, virtually all the student pilots arrived from other regiments, did a flying tour of three years and then returned to life as a soldier. The front-line helicopter then was the Skeeter, 'an appallingly under-powered and hopeless piece of equipment', recalls Shaw. When it was replaced by the Sioux – the Army's name for the Bell 47G3B1 – there was strong pressure to replace the Hillers with the same type, in order to cut down conversion time. 'While accepting the logic of the argument, we were aware of training limitations with the Sioux, especially with its turbocharger and the high-inertia blades, which took longer to stop. We felt that the Bell 47G4A would be a better helicopter for basic training.'

One requirement of a renewed contract was that the selected helicopter should be built in the UK. Initially 50% of the order was given to Agusta and the rest to Westland, which was to assemble them under licence from Italy. However, after lengthy negotiation it was finally agreed that Westland itself would build the BHL B47s, with some British content, under licence from Bell. These helicopters, non-supercharged and with a Lycoming engine, were the only examples of the type that the British firm would ever build.

Each year Alan Bristow would drive down to Middle Wallop in the Rolls-Royce. The staff came to look forward to his visits. He would bring them together, thank them for their hard work over the year and, in the manner of visiting admirals, ask if there were any problems. However this was no cosmetic 'brass hat' exercise. Bristow would act on any complaints there and then and, if he felt a manager wasn't pulling his weight, was quite prepared to deal with the problem right there. He would also act on requests. One year a bowser driver complained of the cold and his lack of warm clothing – a huge Army greatcoat was immediately dispatched.

In 1967 Bryan Shaw was relieved by his chief pilot Doug Batten, who himself was replaced by ex-Spitfire pilot Arthur Sharples. Batten was replaced by Clive Wright, one of the early Air Whaling and North Sea pilots, in 1979. A keen long-distance runner, Clive established the 'Bristow 10' race which he ran each year, accompanied by several keen athletes in the company in preparation for the London Marathon. When he retired in July 1991, the money from the traditional 'whip-round' funded a home gymnasium for his garage. David Mallock took over and supervised the changeover to the Squirrel while Stuart Wakefield, the present incumbent, took on the responsibilities in late 2000.

A Lynx simulator was established in 1979 and BHL provided the instructors for that as well. The three-year support contracts continued through re-negotiation until 1981, when the Bell 47 was replaced by the turbine-powered, Army-owned Gazelle. BHL engineers trained on the new helicopter and took on the maintenance requirements of 658 Squadron Territorial Army. However, once the requirement was reduced to one of 'personnel only', Bristow lost some of its negotiating power. Notwithstanding this, the contract period was later extended to five years.

The year 1981 also saw the formation of the Corps' Historic Aircraft Flight, at the time consisting of a Sioux, a Skeeter and an Auster, which performed air displays during the summer season. A Westland Scout, which served for many years as the Corps' battlefield taxi, joined it in 1984 and an Alouette ten years later. From the beginning BHL has looked after these aircraft, both at MW and whenever they 'overnight' away from base. A Beaver and Chipmunk have since been added and the older types, which are becoming increasingly difficult to keep airborne, get less and

Instructor Tony Collins (callsign 147, in the flight suit) is congratulated on his retirement by, left to right, Commandant Mike Wawn, David Mallock, Chief of Staff Denzil Sharpe, TC, Chief Pilot Bryan Beggs and CFI David Morley.

From one extreme... George Giles with the Historic Flight Skeeter at Bournemouth in the mid-1980s, with Concorde in the background.

less public exposure. At around the same time BHL also donated a Bell 47 to the new Army Air Corps Museum at Middle Wallop.

Engineering Manager Andy McLeod is a particularly fondly-remembered character who, from the mid-1970s to about 1982, looked after the twenty-six Gazelles in Hangar 4. He was a no-nonsense Scot who did not suffer fools gladly. One of his stock phrases was, 'If ye dinna like it laddie, ye know where tae go'. However he never bore a grudge and once he had said his piece, the lads remember, all was forgotten.

Andy's secretary, Carole Collins, found herself accidentally locked inside the hangar with him at one point. He was furious at the inefficiency of it all and she was mortified as to what everyone else might think. Carole left to have a baby in 1981 and several of her successors subsequently became pregnant as well. They blamed the office chair. Undaunted, Carole returned full-time in 1991 and, twelve years later, works as finance co-ordinator.

Buoyed by the early success of this contract, the company started to look farther afield. In 1969 flying instructor Mike Norris flew out to Tehran to discuss, together with base manager Ken Bradley, a plan for establishing a flying training school for the Iranian Gendarmerie, Army and Air Force. This was to be at Ghaleh Morghi, an ex-military airfield in the southern suburbs of the capital. Family commitments meant that Norris was unable to take up the Iranian appointment and, instead, returned to Middle Wallop. Later that year, he was invited to help set up a new training school at Redhill, to satisfy the company's own growing requirements. The Iranian school was established under a joint company – the Iranian Helicopter Aviation Company (IHAC) – and flew eight second-hand, wooden-bladed B47G2s, contributing to the company's growing presence in the country. Charles Walden became the school's first managing pilot, followed by Peter Gray.

Peter Gray recalls that, 'limited power was the name of the game in Iran. I had to ban engine-off landings in the summer because of the high density altitude. The

Galeh Morghi 1977. (Photo John Black)

students completed *ab initio* training on the 47s and then converted to either the Bell 205 or 206 – the Gendarmerie contributed three of each. I remember that mountain training in the nearby Elburz range was particularly rewarding'. The school continued its work until 1976.

Keith Gates, who also served at Galeh Morghi, tells of the diplomatic skills the instructors had to acquire. 'We had one student that needed a full 80 hours before he was ready for first solo. It was almost impossible to fail anyone: the only way was to apologise for *our* failure, for having to teach the course in English, and suggest that the student went for some refresher language training. He would invariably make it in the end, however.'

In 1973, BHL moved into a facility at Exeter Airport, to train the crews from customers who had ordered derivatives of Westland's Sea King. It was run by Pym White. One of these customers was the Egyptian Air Force and the training for those pilots, on their own aircraft, took place at the same time as the Yom Kippur war between Egypt and Israel. Everyone involved kept a very low profile during this period.

Bristow's own vacancies were often filled by pilots from the armed services. Indeed at least one of them, John Willis, joined Bristow after leaving the Royal Navy, where he had been trained in 1961 by BHL at Redhill. However, there were peaks and troughs in this supply. In times of international tension it would drop to a trickle; in relaxed periods, when their skills were less valued and the rewards remained static, more military pilots were tempted by the world 'outside'.

In 1970, at the height of the Cold War, newly appointed operations director Alastair Gordon became aware that, while BHL's requirement for pilots was growing, the supply from the services was drying up. He asked Mike Norris to set up a CAA-approved school at Redhill, using the ex-Middle Wallop Hillers. Alan Bristow's son Laurence was a private student of Mike's during this period, and he acquitted himself well.

At the end of the following year, Mike left for Aberdeen to manage the training for the new S61s. However the school, managed by Stan Sollit and George Bedford, continued to train BHL co-pilots until 1998 on five Robinson R22s. Then its task was contracted out to California-based Helicopter Adventures, under the tutelage of George who set up home in the area. The change was primarily driven by the cheaper operating costs in the USA and, of course, by the better weather. The school has now re-located to Florida.

George Bedford says that the school,

> *simply became a cost centre that Bristow could not afford. With the financial pressure it was under in 1998, it just had to go. I am sure the school had always given good value. It produced a significant number of company pilots who proved, over and over, to be more cost-effective than the majority of qualified pilots.*
>
> *There is no doubt in my mind that, at the time, we ran the Rolls-Royce of flight training schools. My instructors were all experienced offshore pilots and were able to pass on so much more than the basic skills of aircraft handling. The ground school team was second to none, particularly in their experience of helicopter operations.*
>
> *It was a sad day for me when Redhill FTS closed its doors. BHL's commitment to the art of helicopter pilot training had been significant over many years, and remained so up to the end. In the event I believe we have been able to keep the flame alive over here in the US, by reducing costs while maintaining standards. Indeed the company is still committed to a cadet programme, albeit now on a smaller scale.*

Training became a big issue in the mid-1970s, when BHL's accident rate began to rise significantly, especially in areas like Iran, the Persian Gulf and Indonesia. It coincided with efforts to address a pilot shortage. Alastair Gordon identified that the bulk of these accidents were traceable to US ex-Vietnam aviators who, before being sent off to fly various Bell models, had been given fairly cursory competence checks.

David Mallock relieves Clive Wright as base manager in July 1991. Basic rotary wing instructors, left to right, at rear: Sandy Matheson, Gordon Jackson, Dave Randall, Billy Campbell, Jim Bartlett, Alan Wiles, Ian Bell and Paul Shaw. Sitting: Dave Stewart, Ray Elliott, Bryan Beggs, Clive Wright, David Mallock, Tony Collins, Bob Weston and Eddie Ford.

Col. Nigel Thursby (Commandant School of Army Aviation) and Bristow manager David Mallock at the introduction of the AS350 Squirrel to Middle Wallop.

In 1975 Mike Norris was appointed flying training superintendent and invited to use the experience gained in running the successful S61N course in Aberdeen, to introduce a formal, detailed two-week Redhill course for all training captains. He was only in the job a year before being re-appointed as regional flying superintendent for the North Sea, but the accident rate, especially from the pilot error point-of-view, had already begun to fall. A further part of Alastair's efforts to introduce a flight safety culture to the company, led Mike and Bill Petrie being dispatched to take air accident investigator courses in Los Angeles.

By 1995, while BHL was flourishing at MW, the use of civilians to maintain military aircraft continued to expand. However, the process of training naval and Air Force *aircrew* remained very much in-house. As it became clear that, post-Cold War, Britain's armed forces were becoming more occupied with active service, the front line became the focus of much of the uniformed effort. As a result, the Ministry of Defence opted to outsource numerous second line services under 'private finance initiatives'. The first one published, under the banner of the Defence Helicopter Flying School, covered the provision of all basic, and much of the advanced, aircrew flying training.

As a result BHL, joined in consortium with the SERCO manpower agency and FR Aviation, won a fifteen-year contract to provide that training. The main activity was set up at RAF Shawbury in Shropshire, the home of the RAF's Central Flying School, where *ab initio* pilots of all three services now train up to 'Wings' standard. A small detachment was established at RAF Valley on Anglesey, off the North Wales coast, to provide naval and Air Force pilots with search and rescue training.

The tri-service Defence Helicopter Flying School (DHFS) was officially opened at Shawbury on 1 April 1997. It was equipped with a fleet of fourteen Eurocopter AS350BB Squirrels for basic training, six twin-engined Bell 412EP Griffins for advanced, three cockpit procedure trainers representing the Squirrel and a 4-axis dynamic simulator replicating the B412. A mountain flying and SAR detachment at RAF Valley, on the island of Anglesea, operates a further three B412s while another twelve Squirrels are based at Middle Wallop. BHL provides 40% of the flying instructors, all the engineers, plus support services for the manpower and logistic support for the aircraft. Altogether the FBH consortium, now two companies following the SERCO withdrawal, employs over 600 personnel. Courses start every month or so.

The new scheme led to a few redundancies at Middle Wallop – always a painful experience for members of a well-knit team. The MW element of DHFS stands a little separate from the consortium and the Army still refers to it as the School of Army Aviation. Pilots arrive from Shawbury for further operational training on the Squirrels, before starting a conversion to their front-line aircraft.

> *The military still can't believe how we manage to keep our levels of aircraft availability for the price* [says Stuart Wakefield]. *We tell them that they haven't even scratched the surface.*
>
> *I think the introduction of the Apache attack helicopter changes everything. The training centre is currently coming on-line and there's so much to learn. Early students have compared learning about it to trying to drink from a fire-hose, so the idea of de-briefing a sortie at midnight on Saturday is no longer alien.*

Middle Wallop now provides Army pilots with advance training on FBS-owned Squirrels, equipping them for operational conversion onto all the AAC's front-line helicopters – Gazelle, Lynx and eventually Apache too.

The military/civil hybrid has proved extremely successful and the FBH model, of civilian companies taking on the training of military pilots, by a mixture of civil and military instructors on military owned aircraft and under military command, is attracting the interest of the Australian Defence Forces. In another move, the consortium is providing military helicopter support in Cyprus; with four Griffins taking over SAR and utility roles at Akrotiri and Dhekelia on a five-year contract. In 2002, FBH was awarded a contract to supply and support three Bell 212s in Belize. It is to be run in a similar style to a support unit in Brunei, which has been in place since 1994, with Army pilots and Bristow training and engineering support.

This latest initiative may prove to be a turning point in the long-standing argument over who can best provide SAR services in the UK. While BHL has demonstrated that it can provide a service to the same standard as that of the familiar military Sea Kings, yet at a much reduced cost, the Navy and Air Force are reluctant to relinquish valuable training and PR tools. So, the company argues, why not provide COMO (company-owned, military-operated) helicopters, in military livery, flown by a mixture of civil and military crews? The armed forces can keep the kudos and the training value, and BHL can continue to run a successful and cost-effective business.

Watch this space.

## CHAPTER SEVEN

# GLOBAL EXPANSION

In 1963 John Odlin, suffering from complications to a broken nose, asked Alan Green's secretary if she could fix him up with a cheap flight to somewhere warm for a long weekend, where he could get some R&R. He was thinking of Southern France or Spain, perhaps. A few days later Green got him on the phone and said, 'I've found that flight you wanted John – how about Salisbury?' John wasn't impressed. 'What, Salisbury Plain?' 'No, Salisbury Rhodesia.' John thought that was a hell of a long way to go for a long weekend but Alan confessed he had a small job that needed doing there.

'But Alan, I'm supposed to be recuperating.' 'Ah, don't worry about that,' said Green. 'You'll have at least a week before the work starts.'

In fact the six-month job turned out to be all that a young pilot could want – 'a paid-for safari', says Odlin. With support from engineer Tommy Bayden he flew a Hiller 12E around both Northern and Southern Rhodesia, on contract for their Federal Survey. The work involved flying at steady barometric altitudes on 3D mapping sorties, to enable surveyors to map spot heights and contours; and taking teams out to hilltops in the veldt, where they would set up their equipment and take secondary trig readings. Odlin found the work challenging – especially when it came to judging how far he was from home-base. After a few close calls, he took to placing fuel dumps at strategic points in the bush.

They would regularly camp in the bush as well. Hesitant to sleep in the open, especially after one night when an African bearer was carried off by a lion, they took to using a small caravan owned by the Survey. On one occasion the two Britons were sitting around the campfire eating supper, about 200m away from the helicopter. Every night they would be visited by local antelopes that would graze nearby. One night they heard one of the antelopes galloping towards them. Tommy immediately threw his beer in the air and dashed for the caravan, leaving John, somewhat nonplussed, alone in the firelight. After a while, Tommy's face appeared round the door and he plaintively enquired, 'Has it gone?'

Tommy Bayden.

'Tommy, it was only a deer,' said John. 'I know what it was,' came the retort from the caravan. 'It was what was bloody chasing it that bothered me.'

A former RAF Hunter pilot, John Odlin originally joined Pest Control in 1958. After just thirty hours of introduction to helicopters and the Hiller, he had been dispatched to spray acres and acres of bananas – 'as far as the eye could see' – in Panama and the Dominican Republic. He joined an extensive operation where the Hillers, five or six of them at a time, would fly all day and every day. Before long he was accumulating hours at a rate of 1,000 a year, and so had little opportunity to spend his meagre salary – he remembers the barman earned more than he did.

John also met Tommy Bayden in Panama. The engineer's ambitions to fly led him to cadge stick time from his colleagues whenever he could. Over several drinks in a Honduras bar he had talked the visiting ops manager, Dave Bond, into authorising on a beer mat the chief pilot to give him ten hours dual instruction. With that, plus anything else he managed to scrounge, he also managed to talk the local authority into issuing him with a PPL.

Tommy, who had joined Bristow at the time of the Fison merger, eventually upgraded to a CAA commercial licence and became the company's only pilot/engineer combo in Nigeria. 'He was always building hours,' remembers John. 'His aircraft always needed a surprising amount of test flying.'

Before the Rhodesia job, John had also flown from Trinidad, supporting Trinmar (Texaco) oil offshore operations with another Hiller. 'We were based at Antilles, an oilfield accommodation camp next to the famous La Brea Pitch Lake. The Trinmar oilfield was in the Gulf of Paria and named the Soldado Field, after a large rock sat in the middle of the Gulf. I took over from Johnny Johnson, our engineer was Nick Neocleous and the aircraft was a Hiller 12C – originally registered G-APDV but placed on the Trinidad register, as VP-TCE, in April 1961.'

Trinidad Belle 1962. The Hiller is
VP-TCE. (Photo John Odlin)

While John was in Trinidad, Johnny Johnson also flew a piston-engined
Whirlwind for Amoseas, from Balata on the east coast, and later a WS55 and a Bell
47 G2 from the Mayaro airstrip.

A further contract with Dominion Oil developed during the sixties, with a
Whirlwind 3 and a Jet Ranger taking over from the three-seat Hiller, and continues
for BP Amoco to this day. In January 1972 the company purchased a Bell 204B from
Bow Helicopters in Canada (CF-BHB) and John Odlin ferried it to Trinidad from
Calgary, with Chas House as engineer. On arrival it became VR-BED and worked
for Amoco out of Piarco.

After John completed the contract in Rhodesia – he remembers it as 'the job of a
lifetime' – he was posted to Nigeria. This came as something of a culture shock.
Although in these early days, before the Biafran war, Nigeria was still considered an
attractive posting, the unremitting humid heat made for hard work in terms of both
flying and day-to-day living. The oil bonanza was also about to cause severe
sociological and political upheaval, but would make Nigeria Bristow's main profit
centre.

The new job involved a great deal of flying to rigs, both offshore and in the
marshy Niger River delta. At the start of one particularly heavy day, during which
John logged over ten hours, he was called out pre-dawn in his Hiller to fly a casevac
mission. After feeling his way over the jungle and ten miles out to sea, in total
darkness and with no instruments, he located the rig. On the helideck he was
approached by a roughneck, in the care of some handlers, who was nursing a

bandaged thumb. 'I had a bit of a go at them, complaining that they might at least have carried him out here – if only to make me feel it had all been worthwhile. My abiding memory is that the clients, at the time, never seemed to say thank you.'

In 1966 the company bought Dan Pienaar's Helicopter Services of South Africa and, shortly afterwards, formed Helicopteros Portugal Africa Ltd to operate in Mozambique. Jim 'Sharkey' Ward was chief engineer for Helicopter Services and John Cameron was appointed chief pilot to the Mozambique company. The two businesses ran a range of operations, from supplying offshore tankers with provisions as they sailed past Durban, to onshore work such as inspecting power lines. By 1972 they had both been sold to local operator Court Helicopters, but John Cameron came back to BHL.

A contract in Peru for Mobil, headed by John Griffiths – who married a local girl and settled out there – started in 1967 with two Bell 204Bs and lasted nearly three years. This was BHL's introduction to heli-rig work: an operation which involves transporting an entire onshore oil drilling infrastructure, usually far into the jungle where it is inaccessible by other means.

Later in 1967, Bryan Shaw was brought in from running the training school at Middle Wallop, and tasked with looking for new overseas business. He was soon involved in bidding for the company's first operation in the Far East: a heli-rig

Tellerometer work with party at the top of a 1500ft peak, Mozambique 1966.

Offloading survey equipment, Mozambique 1966.

operation in conjunction with Caltex Pacific Indonesia – which would operate under the name of PT Bristow-Masayu Helicopters. Forming this new company in Indonesia took an enormous amount of work and required a great deal of persistence and assistance from its partner Masayu Trading.

The contract was only to be for 180 days and was dependent on BHL obtaining an operating licence in Indonesia. Bryan flew out in January 1968 to look into the process of getting one, but the omens did not seem particularly good. The Sukarno regime had just ended and President Suharto had just taken over. Under the old regime, which had been close to Communist China, Indonesia had been virtually closed to western countries. Furthermore Dutch competitor Schreiner Helicopters thought it had an agreement with Ibno Sutowo, head of state-owned oil company Pertamina, that it should have the operating rights.

During his first visit Bryan, along with only about forty-five fellow guests, stayed at the vast Hotel Indonesia. It would not be long before it would be virtually impossible to get a room there. He first needed to establish who might be responsible for granting the vital operating rights and started, logically, at the Department of Civil Aviation. However he soon realised that quite a few officials each believed it was *he* who had the required authority. After much patient negotiating and hanging around, however, the operating rights were finally granted. Bristow-Masayu Helicopters held the Duri contract that was expected to last 180 days, for a further twenty-five years.

A Bristow-Masayu 'Huey'.

Heli-rigging in action.

Conditions in these early days were not easy. On the day Barry Newman arrived to take up his position as area manager, he had to drive from the airport through a student riot – a riot which was eventually put down by gunfire. Getting from Jakarta to the area of operation was no easier. Jakarta is in Java and the heli–rig operation was in Sumatra, 600 miles away. State airline Garuda was controlled by the military and Bryan's early attempts to travel on it were not always successful. Timetables were moveable feasts and he was advised that his best chance lay in getting to the airport very early in the morning. He tried that twice, both times without securing a seat. The third time he actually got onboard the aeroplane but, at the last minute, was kicked off by an Army officer. The fourth time he secured a place but, at one of the stopping-off points, was again kicked off – by another Army officer. 'It was a tortuous process.'

Odlin flew the very first helicopter in as chief pilot, with Bryan Shaw's words, 'It's only a six-month job John – don't spend any money', ringing in his ears. To play with they had two Jet Rangers (VR–BCR and VR BCQ) and two brand new Bell 205A–1s – VR–BCN and VR–BCO, the first commercial Hueys. However they first had to wait for several months in Singapore, while Bell got the aircraft certified. For a time they also had to make do with under-performing aircraft: certification delays meant that the first few months' work had to be completed using the less powerful Lycoming T53-11 engine.

Huey in action.

Dedicated teamwork and experience. Bell 205 lifting in an accommodation unit, Duri, early 1970s.

*The 'dash 11' engine certainly gave us serious lifting problems with some of the larger items of the Loffland Bros drilling rig. [says John Odlin] The company had developed an air trans-portable rig from their previous experience in Columbia: it had been designed to be dismantled down to loads of 4,000lb, the maximum capable of being slung under a helicopter.*

*Luckily the first jungle rig location, Libo 1, was only 8-10km from the road-accessible staging area. The heavier items were flown both with minimum fuel and at dawn, the coolest part of the day. The 'dash 13' engines arrived and were fitted prior to dismantling the rig and having to fly it out. I recall that it took some three months for Bristow-Masayu to fly in the rig, for Loffland to drill the well and for the helicopters to fly the rig out again. After it had been trans-ported by road to the next helicopter staging area, it was amazing how, from then on, dedicated teamwork and experience was able to substantially reduce the time taken to set up the rig in a new jungle location.*

*We operated the Jet Rangers out of Rumbai, on seismic support before the Bell 205's arrived in early June and we moved to the permanent helicopter base at Duri in central Sumatra, where Caltex built a hangar and Portakabin accommodation for the crews. BHL hired Indonesian pilots and engineers and later set up ab initio training for local trainees.*

'Fred' Dermwan was the first Indonesian pilot. Trained in Russia, he later became the Bristow–Masayu manager. Helicopter registrations were changed over to the Indonesian (PK) Register in December 1968. The two Bell 205A's were delivered by Bell to Singapore in March 1968 and were the first two modified Huey H models to be certified by the FAA.

Bell Jet Ranger, Duri, Indonesia.

*We were keen to see the Duri maintenance hangar built but, when enquiring as to when it might be available, the Caltex planning people admitted they had temporarily lost it within their system. Trying not to sound too pushy with the client, I asked to see the plans. I soon spotted that the door opening was too low, by about a foot, to take the B205. I pointed this out to the American engineer in charge who replied, 'just how long do you intend to have the helicopters in the hangar anyway? We pay you to have them out flying'. I quietly explained that if we could not get them inside at all, they would be both wasting money and failing to meet their contractual obligations. The door opening was modified.*

*We had to make allowances, though. Indonesia was hard work in the early days. We didn't have enough staff and I was having to cajole our people to forego days off, R&R trips to Singapore and so on.*

Many problems had to be overcome but the BHL team's perseverance paid off and soon the company secured further contracts, all in Sumatra, from Mobil, Kennicot, Rio Tinto Zinc and Total. They also won two contracts on Natuna Besar, an island in the South China Sea, one with AGIP – utilising a Sikorsky S61N – and one with Conoco operating two Wessex 60s.

A further contract with International Nickel at Mallili in Sulawesi involved two Bell 206As. Bryan Shaw remembers that one of them went unserviceable. Bill Petrie was also on site and the pair had to work out how to get a spare engine from Macassar Airport to Mallili. They decided that the only way was in a Land Rover, across one of the legs of Sulawesi to the Gulf of Bonny and then by boat up the Gulf.

An emerging jungle landing strip near Duri, Indonesia.

The two set off, along an appalling road. The country had been suffering levels of conflict since 1938 and every single bridge had been blown. Eventually they reached the Gulf, where a launch sent by International Nickel was waiting. They were now faced with the problem of transferring the engine on to the launch, which had too deep a draught to come alongside the bank. They somehow managed it by using a canoe. Then the skipper would not set off because the tide was wrong. Eventually the tide was right but by then it was also dark and, afraid of attack, the skipper would not travel at night. Bryan and Bill used their powers of persuasion, and all their available cash, until at last they were off. Then the boat's engine stopped. Petrie got it going and they finally delivered their valuable cargo.

Bryan Shaw recalls that, at the time, everything in Indonesia was primitive and not a little frightening. 'Communication was difficult at best, and often impossible. We resorted to making blind radio position reports, in the hope that someone would pick them up.'

Jungle bases in Indonesia would attract wildlife of all shapes and sizes and the crews, in grand British tradition, tried to domesticate many of them. Some species, sloths and alligators for example, posed particular challenges and yet the men at the Duri camp tried to adopt examples of both species. One waif, a baby orang-utan they took in and christened Judy, proved a more successful rearing. Judy was hand-reared, on boiled milk fed to her through an eye-dropper, and kept in a box lined with cotton wool. She repaid the men's kindness and, some months after being returned to the wild, re-appeared with a baby of her own.

This success went to the Duri men's heads and, for their next venture, they took on a tiger cub. As with Judy, it was tiny when found and needed feeding from an eye dropper. Once again, the animal thrived and quickly grew into a very playful young tiger. It was when she reached the size of a large Alsatian, and showed no signs of arresting her growth, that the Duri Doolittles decided that perhaps she would be better off in the wild.

Between January and October 1970, a Bristow team operated a Series 3 Whirlwind (PK-HBM) in support of Union Carbide, drilling for oil off the east coast of Borneo in the Macassar Straits and Masalembo, Indonesia, an island between Java and Borneo. Chief Engineer Frank Chammings recalls that,

*About twice a week, the Whirlwind took off from Masalembo for Surabaya where it picked up passengers and freight from the Jakarta DC9. It then flew to Masalembo for refuelling and then to Pualu Laut, an island off the south-east corner of Borneo where we had set up a refuelling stop and then to the drilling ship run by Zapata. The trip from Masalembo and back took seven and a half hours and, at the time, had to be the longest operational run for a single-engined helicopter anywhere in the world.*

*The refuelling stop at Pulau Laut meant hand-pumping drums of Jet A1, which had been transported to the island by workboat and underslung by helicopter to the location. On one occasion the helicopter shut down for lunch, while Ian Dobson and I were on the MV Millentor – a German-crewed workboat. After eating, we waited for the helicopter to finish uplifting the drums but we could see, through the trees, that the rotors still weren't turning.*

*After a while we realised that the crew were on the beach trying to attract our attention so we asked the captain to launch the tender. Its engine wouldn't start and it took an age to get going until, eventually at nightfall, we got the crew aboard with the 55's flat batteries. The boat was*

Duri, Indonesia, in 1970.

*short of rations so we only had a fried egg each for supper – Ian D loved his food and was much put out. The batteries were charged up overnight; we eventually got the aircraft started and made straight back to Masalembo, leaving the fuel drums on the boat.*

Burmah Oil was beginning to explore off the north-western coast of Australia and, in 1967, BHL sent a Wessex 60 (G-AVEW) and a crew out to support its work. An Australian partner was required and the operation was set up with a Melbourne-based transport company called Mayne-Nickless Pty.

The first Mayne-Bristow Wessex was shipped from the UK – the packing crate reportedly ended up in great demand as a beach hut – and flown from Perth up to Broome by Ian Clark, together with engineers Bernie Rose and Ray Knight. A second pilot, Keith Gates, joined him there. Ian recalls that, 'the multi-racial township of Broome – population 1,500 – was at the time the crowded, colourful and rowdy centre of the Australian pearl industry'. Keith recalls suffering his worst-ever hangover, drinking sake and beer with a group of Japanese pearl fishermen.

In September 1967, the crew prepared the helicopter for operations from Broome. The Wessex had originally been intended for a job in colder climes and Keith remembers that, apart from a long-range fuel tank, it boasted a highly efficient cabin heater which would clearly be less than useless in the Australian climate. As well as removing it, Bernie and Ray cut a hole in the floor and fitted a scoop to direct 'fresh' air into the cabin. By early October, it was ready to start earning its keep.

Once cleared by the Australian DCA to fly in the 46°C heat, the Wessex began the task of supplying offshore drilling vessel *Investigator*, which was sinking Burmah Oil's first wildcat well off Western Australia. Floating in the Timor Sea on the edge of the Ashmore Reef, the *Investigator* lay over 360 nautical miles north of Broome. The longest sector was 143nm, which entailed careful flight planning by the Bristow crews. Remote refuelling stations were set up along the route, at Cape Leveque and on two coral atolls known as Browse and Adele Island. The refuelling task was routinely undertaken by the pilot, with the help of passengers who had been 'detailed off'. The drums of fuel were occasionally tapped or even removed by passing fishermen and this pilfering led, on several occasions, to off-the-cuff revisions to the flight plan.

Initially they flew with two crew but dispensation was soon obtained from the DCA for single-pilot operations. They kept in HF contact with Broome or Darwin through a trailing aerial – similar to the one Alan Bristow had deployed in the Antarctic, nearly twenty years before – and NDBs set up at the refuelling points would hopefully help with navigation.

*We started flying single pilot and changed the rig crews round twice weekly. [Says Keith Gates] We were soon taking on extra flights and, after our individual hour rates grew to over 100 a month, Dave Eckersley and Dick Tudor were recruited to help and we reverted to twin-pilot operations. The long flights were further complicated by the uncertain weather conditions, as the whole area lies in the Australian cyclone belt. Between December and February winds in excess of 100mph can sweep across the route. Nevertheless, flying continued with the help of Darwin Met, which could accurately plot the courses of cyclones and give shipping and aircraft ample forewarnings.*

A Mayne-Bristow Wessex lifts out a bent Airfast Hiller.

One day, despite Met forecasts, the helicopter's route took it through the edge of a cyclone. The rain on the windscreen soon became so fierce that Keith and Dick had to take it in turns to fly with their heads poking out of an open side-window. They had good HF contact but the NDBs were useless in the storm, so they missed the first refuelling point, landing on the *Investigator* with minimal fuel. Just after taking off again, full to the gunwales with jet fuel, they suffered an engine failure.

They were far too heavy to land on the rig again so Keith ran the Wessex on to a nearby beach at Ashmore Reef. The weather soon improved and a boat was dispatched from the rig to evacuate the passengers. Keith, on the other hand, had no alternative but to take off again with the one remaining engine, turn back and make for Adele Island through the tail-end of the storm. Another single-engine landing later and Keith and Dick flopped onto the beach on their backs, arms and legs outstretched, discussing the thought that they might both be getting too old for this sort of thing.

Incidentally, this engine failure happened on a Friday. The detachment notified Redhill and the engineering department swung into action. A replacement was air-freighted out to them in time for the Wessex to fly again on the Monday. The crew had been hoping for more of a break.

EW was eventually lost in a fire aboard the *Investigator*. While Dave Eckersley was drinking coffee below decks, a large lump of smouldering soot found its way into the cockpit and set it alight. Dave hot-footed it from the galley to find his helicopter in flames. Soon afterwards, in June 1969, a second helicopter (G-AWXX), flown by

Ian Clark and Tony English, made its own way to Australia. The epic journey from Redhill to Port Samson took seventeen days and 11,184 miles: for a long time it held the record for the longest-ever helicopter flight.

Mayne-Bristow became established at Karratha Airport in Western Australia in 1973, when the first of two permanent hangers were built. As demands for its services grew, especially from Woodside, a third hanger was added in 1981.

The Puma was operated as the fleet mainstay from 1979: the first one was an ex North Sea aircraft G-BFSV (VH-BHO). The fleet increased to five and at one stage was ferrying 1,200 passengers a week between Karratha and offshore installations. Bell 212s were imported for general utility work and to back-up the Pumas. The Agusta-Bell 206s were naturally used on smaller jobs, including geo-survey work and harbour master duties.

The Mayne-Nickless company sold its stake in the business in 1991 but the contract continues to this day under the banner of Bristow Helicopters Australia. A Super Puma operation also flies from Darwin, for Woodside Petroleum, 250 miles to a rig in the Zone of Co-operation between Australia and Indonesia. 'It remains a very sound operation', says Chris Fry. Chris, son of George Fry, spent over thirty years in senior commercial positions with the company.

SA33OJ Puma on finals.

Mayne-Bristow Super Pumas at Karratha, Western Australia.

B212, Australia.

*Previous page:* 1. Bristow Tiger.

*Above:* 2. Gazelle.

*Opposite above:* 3. Bell 47G2. (Photo Malcolm Pendrill)

*Opposite below:* 4. Bell 47G4A.

*Above:* 5. DHFS Squirrels.

*Opposite above:* 6. A 4-axis dynamic simulator replicates the B412 at RAF Shawbury.

*Opposite below:* 7. 'The Rolls-Royce of flight schools'. R22s in formation. (Photo Malcolm Pendrill)

*Above:* 8. Bell 212, Trinidad.

*Opposite above:* 9. One of the first BHL S61Ns operated out of Kuala Trengganu, Malaysia.

*Opposite below:* 10. The S61N.

11. 'I know it's cheaper, JR, but is it cost effective!?' (Copyright: Tugg, 1982-2003)

12. SA330J Puma.

13. The Portland SAR S61N.

14. 'Project Jigsaw' Super Puma.

15. Coastline search.

16. G-BIMU, Stornoway SAR.

*Previous page:* 17. Bright orange stripes for visibility.

*Above:* 18. Zigzag rope encircles the hull of every Bristow S61N.

*Opposite above:* 19. Mount Pleasant Airport under construction in the Falklands. (Photo Paul Boland)

*Opposite below:* 20. Winter logistics in the Falklands.

*Above:* 21. Bell 212, UN Logistics, Kosovo. (Photo Roger D. Smith)

*Opposite above:* 22. Bristow Australia Ltd. (Photo Ron Israel)

*Opposite below:* 23. Tiger formation.

*Overleaf:* 24. Standing by on a helideck.

Bob Balls (left) and engineer Ken Rowe flew this Wessex from London Gatwick to Kuala Lumpur. The 8,600-mile flight took eighteen days.

Bristow's activity in Malaysia had first started in 1968, with Whirlwind 3s operating on behalf of Esso from bases at Kuala Trenganu, Kuantan and later Kerteh. They needed upgrading so the oil company reserved slots on Sikorsky's production line for two new S61Ns: without knowing at the time who would be operating them on its behalf. On the evening the order was made the local Sikorsky rep, overwhelmed by the commission he was about to receive, was observed getting extremely drunk in the bar of Kuala Lumpur's Merlin hotel. Bristow, or more accurately Bristow Helicopters Malaysia Sdn Bhd, won the contract, financed the airframes through Bermuda and started flying them in February 1970 – the first time the workhorse S61N appeared in BHL colours. Four new S76s followed and, in the late 1970s, BH Malaysia won a Shell contract to operate four Puma Js, together with an HS125 to link with the capital and two Twin Otters, from Miri in Sarawak.

In 1970 Mike Norris and Hans Schultz undertook a seven-month geological survey of the river system in Sumatra, for Kennecot Mining, flying two newly-acquired Bell 206A Jet Rangers from jungle camps. Weather and communications difficulties played an important part in this contract – on one occasion Schultz was forced down by a thunderstorm, miles from home, and it was twenty-four hours before Norris got the news that both he and his helicopter were safe and well.

Bell 206, Muarabeliti, South Sumatra, May 1973.

Management had to be put in place to make the most of all these international opportunities and, in particular, to procure the best aircraft for each contract. In March 1970 Alan Green was appointed market research director, Alastair Gordon operations director, Bryan Collins commercial director and Bill Mayhew administration director. However Alan Bristow feels that an element of the success and growth that BHL achieved in the 1970s sprang from his own ability to look ahead.

> I persuaded British & Commonwealth and Sir Nicholas Cayzer to take the view that we had to buy ahead, in anticipation of market demand. George Fry and I were very positive in that policy. We should try to order equipment to take advantage of an expanding market ten years down the line. It is dangerous to try and look beyond then but, in the late sixties, I kept on stressing to my colleagues that that's what we needed to do. With full board support I was able to buy ahead of the market, so we always had equipment available, at relatively short notice, to put us in a position to both tender and fulfil our contract obligations.

Alan Green was the first of the Air Whaling 'originals' to die, prematurely, in 1972. Bryan Collins remembers him as a man of integrity who was unfailingly loyal to his friends and colleagues. 'He was also very good with customers, especially those in the Middle East. For several years we couldn't go wrong in the Persian Gulf, as long as Alan was involved.'

'He was a fantastic personality,' says John Odlin. 'Everybody liked Alan. He had the knack of being able to persuade pilots to go anywhere and, within reason, do anything. He may not have been the smartest administrator going – his secretary Eileen Gallagher could help him in that department – but he kept all the operations manned around the world. He effectively ruled our lives and he looked after us well. If you had any problems of any kind, he was the man to go to.'

CHAPTER EIGHT

# THE FLYING TIGERS

As North Sea oilfields continued to be developed during the 1970s, BHL customers demanded that their people be flown, in ever-greater numbers, to points in the ocean at ever-increasing ranges from land. John Odlin, by now Aberdeen base manager, remembers that in their haste to get the stuff ashore, they effectively 'threw money' at their suppliers.

'Time was everything,' he says. 'They didn't have aviation departments: if an oil company needed another helicopter the general manager would throw you a contract which effectively read, "Dear Bristow, please supply an S61 for such-and-such an oil company by Monday", and you would try and find another helicopter in time'. As the Beryl and Brae platforms were taking shape, modules were added *in situ* and accommodation rigs – or 'floatels' – moored up alongside. At any one time there could easily be 2,000 people working on each platform, almost all of whom needed bringing in and out by helicopter.

This increase in activity precipitated a move to larger and more sophisticated aircraft. Pilots had been flying the Wessex 60 since 1965 and, in the early days, the Westland workhorse had given good service. It had true single-engine performance and, due to specially modified engine air intakes, was cleared for flight in icing conditions.

However, in the light of rapid technological advance and the increasing number of roles required of it, the Wessex began to look increasingly unsophisticated. BHL's main competition, British European Airways Helicopters, had been quick to recognise the potential of Sikorsky's S61N. The twin-engined machine had a comparatively vast eighteen/twenty-four-seat cabin – the Wessex could take a maximum of sixteen over a relatively short range – and advanced avionics which enabled it to make automatic, hands-off approaches.

When the first Bristow S61N entered North Sea service in 1971, the company was moving into its first premises on the western perimeter of the airfield. By 1975, the helicopter was the mainstay of BHL's Scottish fleet, with as many as twenty-three of them based at Aberdeen and Sumburgh, on South Shetland.

Hangars for the Sumburgh operation were built between 1975 and 1978 and, shortly thereafter the airport authority built a new terminal to cater for this growing business. However, in an effort to quickly recoup its investment, the CAA airport management decided to charge the helicopters almost Heathrow-style rates for the privilege of landing and staying there. This was the main reason why, by the eighties, most of the business had shifted to Unst, the northernmost of the Shetlands.

Until then, the airfield on the north of Unst had served only to ease pressure at Sumburgh. Any S61N crew unlucky enough to draw the straw for the 'heavy chevy' run – a double run to Chevron's Ninian Field – could expect to be in their seats for over seven hours each day, and the duty would last for several days. Scheduling officer Magnus Bentley says, 'they would take off from Sumburgh at 0730, fly empty with an engineer to the Ninian, pick up fuel and a load of passengers and fly them into Unst, so that they could connect with a Twin Otter service back to Aberdeen. Finally, the helicopter crew would return to Sumburgh. It was a long old day'.

By 1978 Chevron was intent on developing Unst into a proper helicopter base. Three S61Ns and two 330J Pumas were based there and BHL built a hangar and five bungalows on the airfield's perimeter.

A training centre was already in place at North Denes in Norfolk but, with the S61N now at Aberdeen, a new one was required. It was originally set up in an old wartime office block: then moved into Portakabins outside what is now the 'heavy hangar', before moving to the present-day 'H' block. Training was supplemented by flight time that BHL bought on an S61N simulator, which British Airways Helicopters had acquired. The ground-school was originally managed by 'Taff' Evans, a veteran pilot of overseas operations. A simple Link trainer, set up in the heavy hangar at about the same time, helped ex-service pilots practice the procedures necessary for offshore operations.

In April 1977, over fifty pilots initiated a damaging strike in Aberdeen, an event which Philip Warcup later referred to as a 'watershed' in the company's history. The pilots had become angry about their pay and conditions, especially compared with their counterparts from British Airways Helicopters (formerly BEAH), and also wanted to draw attention to a general impression that the management at Redhill were not attuned to their interests. Pilots union BALPA had also managed to gain a foothold in the company – a development that was guaranteed to upset Alan Bristow.

Ultimately, however, the catalyst for the strike was a single pilot, a BALPA member, who refused to take up an appointment in Nigeria before his tour on the North Sea had ended. This refusal was taken extremely seriously by operations director Alastair Gordon, who felt he was quite within his rights to make the appointment. The young man was on the point of being summarily dismissed until he rallied the support of a recently-established local pilot group and, later, pilots' union BALPA. Together, they threatened industrial action in his support.

There followed a period of hectic negotiations, during which Alan Bristow and his senior team flew up to address the staff face-to-face. Although he refused to talk to the union, Bristow did go some way to address the pilots' concerns, to the extent that a way around the problem appeared to be within reach. Unfortunately a

S61N landing on the *Western Pacesetter* platform.

combination of misunderstanding, intransigence and 'goalpost shifting' meant that the strike was eventually called, and picket lines were established outside the Aberdeen base.

While seventeen of the concerned pilots decided not to join the action, over fifty did and were soon dismissed. To fill the gaps, pilots were brought in from overseas and from management tasks at Redhill. Unionised BAH joined the strike and, bizarrely, non-striking BHL crews found themselves having to cover for their work as well. More worryingly the fuel tanker drivers, staunch unionists to a man, refused to cross picket lines and precipitated a severe shortage of aviation fuel. After a frantic series of negotiations over several days, Jack Woolley managed to find 500,000 gallons in Rotterdam. He had it tankered to non-unionised Felixstowe and hired his own drivers to bring it to Aberdeen.

The arrival of this fuel was the pivotal incident which, eventually, caused the strike to fizzle out. With replacement aircrews in place, the loyalty of the engineers and support staff, and enough fuel for the helicopters, BHL's operation was able to continue. Nevertheless, it took several months for the pilots who had been brought in to cover for the strikers to be able to return to their regular appointments.

The dispute split families down the middle. One pilot stayed flying, while his brother went on strike and was fired. Friendships were shattered. Wives refused to speak to other wives. Strikers crossed the road to avoid meeting non-strikers. A mutual feeling of betrayal between pilots and management lingered for years afterwards.

The head of the subsequent inquiry, Lord McDonald, criticised everyone involved.

> This dispute ... would not have happened if parties had acted reasonably throughout. The initial fault lay with the company for failing to appreciate the strength of feeling among their pilots at Aberdeen and to provide a satisfactory channel of communication for this feeling to be expressed. The company was also at fault for insisting that the pilot accept a posting away from Aberdeen when they had no power under his contract so to do.
>
> The other dismissed pilots were at fault for trying to seek their own solutions by taking industrial action. The legal remedies which exist ... are designed to meet this type of situation and are adequate. They are also at fault for not accepting the offer which was made to them [just before the strike started].
>
> Thereafter blame for failure to terminate the strike more quickly must be shared by the company, the striking pilots and BALPA. The actions of BALPA officials in involving other unions and organisations, on inadequate and misleading information, caused the dispute to escalate in a way that should never have happened.

Finally, Lord McDonald censured Alan Bristow.

> [He] is a colourful if controversial figure well known to both sides of industry. He has a turn of phrase more suited to the barrackroom than the boardroom. His talents as an entrepreneur command admiration, and for these he is respected by his employees. At the same time many fear him. In the modern industrial world that type of relationship is not a sure foundation for business success.
>
> He must bear much of the blame for allowing the dispute to begin in the first instance. An intelligent man, he saw at an early stage that he might be wrong and thereafter, by his various efforts, went a long way to have the dispute terminated. He does not, however, understand the art of communication – except in basic terms – and it was largely for that reason that his efforts ... did not succeed.

The primary legacy of the strike, however, would be to make both BHL and its customers realise they could make do with less. The oil companies, until then used to having at least one helicopter on immediate standby for anything they might require, realised that if they stuck to a scheduled service they could negotiate cheaper contracts. In time, passenger loads were consolidated to provide high load factors and freight deliveries were arranged to arrive 'just in time' by sea.

The way of doing business in the North Sea would eventually reflect this new mood. At the time, however, activity quickly returned to normal and continued to grow. Two years later, during the month of June 1979, 19,000 aircraft movements were recorded in the Brent Field alone. Although many of the sectors involved – shuttle flights between platforms – lasted no longer than two minutes, it was a higher figure than that achieved during the same month at London's Heathrow Airport.

During this offshore heyday, there were times when the routine of supporting such a high tempo of operations benefits from a little light relief. Les Kemp, who worked in BHL's Sumburgh office, thought it could do with some, while the strike was on its last legs.

*During the Queen's Silver Jubilee celebrations in June 1977, our chief pilot Terry Wolfe-Milner decided to put a couple of aircraft on the apron on the Sunday for the locals to have a look at. He asked airport manager Les Isaacs if he had any objections: he had none and so a brief announcement was placed in the* Shetland Times.

*Other operators then showed interest. BAH offered to put an S61N on display and demonstrate water landings in the sea. Regional airlines Loganair, Dan Air and Peregrine offered to do some fly-pasts. Between Tuesday, when the idea was conceived, and Sunday, when it took place, a mini air show was arranged. Les Isaacs suggested that someone should give a running commentary, using a loudhailer. He also suggested that I should be that commentator: an idea which horrified me but which was soon seized upon by others.*

*On the Sunday, before the show started, a quick visit to the Sumburgh Club for Dutch courage ended up with Les Isaacs sending whiskies along the bar to me, in an attempt to enliven my part in the proceedings. They didn't help my clarity of speech so, after I had struggled through a nightmare of a commentary, I started thinking of how I might get my own back.*

*Two days later Jubilee celebrations were to climax at Westminster Abbey, with a service attended by the Queen and Commonwealth Heads of States. Uganda's dictator Idi Amin, although having been told he would not be welcome, had announced his intention of attending. He then disappeared from the public eye but continued to be a hot topic in the press.*

*On the big day I had the idea of faking a telex to Isaacs, suggesting that Amin was thought to be making his way from Norway to Sumburgh; from there to travel to London for the service. I gave Amin all his self-appointed titles –  His Excellency Field Marshal Idi Amin Dada, VC and so on – in the outlandish style of language used, at the time, by the humorist Alan Coren in his popular* Punch *magazine column. The telex carried the Foreign & Commonwealth Office telex number and 'callback' – which I found in the directory – and I made up a tape to look authentic. Bear in mind that, by now, there was no way Amin could have reached London in time to take part in the celebrations.*

Bristow flew Margaret Thatcher during her 1979 election campaign.

*I carried on working as it was a busy day. On many occasions I had to call the tower to file flight plans and, each time, a laughing air trafficker would ask if that flight was commanded by Capt. Harnes-Barnes, or whatever fictitious name I had used on the telex. I took for granted that they knew that I had sent the telex and seen it for what it was.*

*Later I sent another one, again purporting to be from Idi Amin, to the effect that he had diverted to Fair Isle. The next thing I knew, two plain clothes policemen had marched in and accused me of sending the messages. I immediately denied all knowledge but they found a black plastic bag, containing all the paper scrap, so I had to confess. I was summarily arrested and had to hurriedly call someone in to take over. I was taken to Lerwick and, to my disgust, put in a cell for the night.*

*Appearing before the Sheriff the next morning, I was charged with public mischief. It turned out that in response to my telex the Home Secretary, together with various other dignitaries, had been called out of Westminster Abbey. Apparently, since no one knew where Amin was, an instruction had been issued that any communication concerning him – even if it was thought to be a hoax – had to be reported. Almost every Shetland police officer was armed and sent to the airport, in case he did turn up. The terminal was apparently full with policemen mingling with the oil workers. The SAS were put on alert to fly to Sumburgh and the Chief Constable, based in Inverness, had a charter flight put on standby.*

*The Sheriff was extremely boot-faced but the Procurator Fiscal (prosecuting) had the grace to laugh as he was reading the spoof telexes, aloud in court. Having already pleaded guilty I was lectured by the Sheriff and fined £100.*

*A whip-round was organised at the airport and I also received a couple of pounds, anonymously, from readers of the* Shetland Times *where the story featured prominently. As a result the fine was paid for by others but I still had to pay legal costs, together with the cancellation charge for the aircraft chartered by the Chief Constable.*

*One of our clients sent me a bottle of whisky and I heard later that Alan Bristow, advised of my arrest by Terry, had told him to bail me out and pay the fine if necessary. Bail had been refused – they were obviously worried that I might slip the country.*

Notwithstanding all the North Sea activity, helicopter operators were unable to argue a case with Aberdeen Airport for specific, helicopter-orientated procedures. Although they were by far the largest users of the airport, especially in the early days when the only fixed-wing service was a daily Viscount flight from London, the air traffic service refused to countenance anything other than helicopter approaches to the main runway or, in the right conditions, to the cross-wind strip. As the amount of aeroplane traffic also grew, their case gradually weakened and, since the oil companies were paying for

The management team, March 1976. From left, sitting: Hans Strasser, Mike Ratcliffe, Bob Roffe, Bob Brewster, John Odlin, George Fry, Alan Bristow, Jack Woolley, Alastair Gordon, Philip Warcup, Colin Agombar, Chuck Bond, John Willis, Doug Batten, Ernie Perrin. Standing: John Griffith, Dave Barber, Ian Clark, Clive Wright, Bryan Shaw, Chris Fry, Laurence Bristow, Bryan Collins, John Howard, Bill Mayhew, Bill Petrie, John Hall and Joe Balint.

the extra flying involved anyway, in the end they gave up trying. 'We even tried to let them give us our own strip,' says John Odlin, 'but they weren't interested.'

In 1978 BHL took over British Executive Air Services (BEAS), a small operator supporting offshore-based B212s and with overseas operations in Libya. Its staff were absorbed into the BHL organisation and its helicopters continued working offshore, so causing little discernible effect on Aberdeen operations. BEAS' Coventry headquarters was closed and some of its staff also joined BHL.

In 1980 the Sikorsky S76, known in the early days as the Spirit, entered service. Initially four of these aircraft were based at Aberdeen, making BHL the first European operator to put this second-generation type into commercial service. Following early problems encountered in bringing this particular type into service (Chapter 12), the helicopter eventually found its spiritual home in North Denes.

The company had by now been having trouble with its Wessex fleet; losing as many as four in unrelated fatal accidents. This was before the days of flight data recorders and BHL was the only civil operator of the type. The last straw came with the unexplained loss of G-ASWI in August 1981, after which Alan Bristow insisted that Westland take them all back again.

From extremely humble origins, then, the Bristow presence at Aberdeen and over the North Sea grew enormously. Between 1972 and 1982 the expansion of personnel at Aberdeen was almost a hundred-fold; despite this staff turnover was, by local standards, relatively low. In addition to 235 pilots, the northern North Sea bases employed 300 people on aircraft maintenance, planning and administration. By the mid-1980s BHL was the airport's largest single employer and ran the greater part of North Sea operations. BAH ran Sumburgh and a few Aberdeen aircraft and a new player – Bond Helicopters (formerly North Scottish) – was providing strong competition after cutting its teeth on inter-rig shuttle services.

Towards the end of this period, the company's overseas commitments, such as Egypt, Indonesia and the Persian Gulf, were contracting. Alan Bristow, concerned that spare engineering capacity was growing at Redhill, decided that BHL should offer its expertise, as a separate technical services business, to civil and military helicopter operators around the world. Alastair Gordon and commercial manager Allan Brown subsequently nominated engineer Chas Newport to take on this new responsibility, to compete with well-established customers such as Motorflug, Ostermans and Singapore Aerospace.

Chas decided that the Persian Gulf, where the Bristow name was well known and respected, was the best place to start. He managed to secure a meeting with a colonel in the Dubai Air Force, who he had heard was not happy with the service he was getting. He met the officer and was swiftly asked to prepare a proposal, to overhaul the dynamic components of his Bell helicopters. While in the region he decided to visit the ex-Bristow chief engineer of Gulf Helicopters at Doha, with whom BHL had been working for some years.

He also asked for a quotation and, not long after his return, Chas heard that both his proposals had been accepted. He soon needed an assistant and took on Colin Miller as the division's level of business and, before long, its reputation began to

S76 landing on.

blossom. During 1984, its first year of trading, the department turned over about half a million pounds. By 1987 this had increased dramatically, matching those of the specialist overhaul shops which had been in place for years.

New business in Europe followed, notably in Norway and Yugoslavia, and then in South America and Africa. Customers in many of these countries had to be convinced that, for major inspections, their aircraft did not have to be returned to the manufacturer. At its peak in the late eighties, the division was supporting as many as 300 third-party helicopters worldwide.

In the spring of 1982, the most sophisticated helicopter ever seen over the North Sea came into service – the Aerospatiale 332L Super Puma. BHL had been operating eleven of the earlier Pumas 'Js', the civil version of the Air Force F model, which had been bought from Aerospatiale for a particularly good price, as a stop-gap to cover shortages in S61N production.

A solitary Bolkow Bo105 was contracted to support lighthouse operations.

Aberdeen with Tigers and S61N.

At the Boeing factory in October 1979. Left to right: Bill Mayhew, Alan Bristow, Bryan Collins and Andrew Muriel (company secretary and lawyer).

*We didn't particularly rate them* [says Bryan Collins] *but their capacity and performance were OK, if we operated them from Sumburgh and we needed something in a hurry. Shell in particular was keen to minimise the time its employees spent over-water in a helicopter, and the Puma worked well in the payload-range equation. We also used the S58ET as a stop-gap but its single-engine performance was questionable, while the Puma had power to spare.*

*George Fry ordered the first three Pumas Js on spec − a request which caused the French manufacturer some discomfort − with options on another eight. We didn't have the work for them at the time but we were confident that something would turn up. Life was like that in those days.*

*In 1982 we also suffered a fatal Puma J training accident at Aberdeen, following which the aircraft rolled over and leaking fuel from the sponson fuel tanks caught fire. From then onwards we decided that we would not fly helicopters without crashworthy external tanks.*

Technical director Jack Woolley retired soon after the first Super Puma arrived. At the time he was responsible for exactly 1,020 engineers − a far cry from when, at Henstridge, he did all the jobs himself. The company was also operating 155 helicopters and eleven aeroplanes. Jack took with him one of the lathes he had first bought for Air Whaling in 1953 − and which he soon restored to full working order.

By now British Airways Helicopters had ordered Boeing's civil BV234 Chinook, a forty-four-seater which could also reach the Brent Field direct from Aberdeen. Although BHL directors made several visits to Philadelphia, they remained unconvinced of Boeing's operating and overhaul cost projections for the massive helicopter, and demanded performance guarantees. These were not forthcoming − Bryan Collins remembers one Boeing executive lamely answering all their questions with, 'I hear you' − so a provisional order for five helicopters started to fall apart.

*Above:* Alan Bristow accepts the keys to the first Bristow Tiger, Marseilles, 12 March 1982.

*Below:* George Fry ordered the first three Pumas on spec.

*Left:* Jack Woolley, 1979.

The Bristow delegation at Marseilles, March 1982.

There were also practical considerations, as not all Brent helidecks could accommodate the twin-rotored Chinooks. Bryan also recalls a hesitation held by some of the BHL team at the time, concerning the idea that a forty-four-passenger payload perhaps constituted too many eggs for one basket. There was also some question over its usage: the most that Chinooks were being asked to fly at the time was around seventeen hours a month, while BHL would demand ten hours a *day*. In the end, Alan Bristow made the decision not to go any further.

BHL executives had meanwhile seen some drawings and specs for the proposed AS332 Super Puma, and went to work on them. In return for an order, including options, for thirty-five of the new helicopters, Bristow demanded space for baggage stowage behind the cabin, a more flexible seating system, customised avionics, bigger windows and better flotation devices.

The order for what was essentially a new variant was placed early in 1981. At over $100 million it was, at the time, the largest civil helicopter order ever made, and it dominated production at Aerospatiale's Marignane plant, in southern France, for a full two years. The first of what Alan Bristow christened 'Tigers' was handed over on 12 March 1982 at Marignane, and immediately flown back to Redhill for the installation of custom avionics and fitting out of the cabin interior. Seven S61Ns, which were sold to Aerospatiale in part-exchange, remained in BHL's Sumburgh hangar for several years afterwards.

Alan Bristow insisted on the new name for a number of reasons. It was to recognise the custom-designed comm/nav systems, redesigned seating and passenger entertainment system on which they had insisted. On the avionics side the refinements included a Decca RNAV, VHF marine radio, colour radar, and a cockpit instrument panel refined from its substantial North Sea experience. There were a grand total of thirty-four improvements over the original helicopter. They included dispensing with a toilet which was sited in the forward left-hand side of the cabin, in full view of the passengers, and with only a flimsy curtain around it. Burly oil-workers in bulky immersion suits generally preferred to hang on until they got to their destination.

Equally important, though, was the idea that they should dissociate the aircraft from those perceived negative traits that the earlier Puma J models had exhibited: in particular the narrow undercarriage and tall fuselage, which made it unstable on the ground in strong winds. It wasn't too popular with the passengers either: its early centre-line troop-style seating and lack of windows had led many to dub it the 'Spewma'.

The ideas and expertise behind the Tiger modifications represented a classic marketing exercise by Alan Bristow. From the very outset of the programme, the company consulted the oil industry about what features they wanted in a helicopter: much of its input was included in the operational aircraft design. For one thing, the interior of the Tiger, while less roomy than the S61N, was designed for comfort to reduce passenger fatigue. Its cabin vibration levels were much lower. Of paramount

Tiger at the Bridge of Don, Aberdeen 1980s.

Bristow-designed
seating for the Tiger.

importance, however, was the fact that the Tiger could make the journey from
Aberdeen to the Thistle Field in one two-hour leg, thus reducing both working time
lost in travel and passenger – and crew – fatigue. The oil companies could begin to look
upon being marooned beneath the Sumburgh summer sea fogs as a thing of the past.

Bristow was also determined that each of his Tigers should be exactly the same as
the others, with no more discrepancies between avionics, cockpit layout or
performance specification. Although a few odd-balls, acquired from overseas, have
crept in over the years, all the 'TIG'-registered aircraft, representing 95% of the fleet,
remain identical.

Before long, one oil company executive was moved to comment: 'in the past I
think too many manufacturers have tried to get us to tailor our needs, as customers,
to an aircraft's capability "as-seen". This, within certain limits, gets it the wrong way
around, so the Bristow approach is very welcome. The fact that so many Tigers are
on order indicates a huge degree of industry approval.'

In any event, the first Tiger arrived at Aberdeen on 9 April 1982 and went into
service, exactly on schedule, for the British National Oil Corporation in the Thistle
Field. As things turned out it was not a perfectly smooth introduction. An unduly
high rotor blade pitch led to uncomfortable vibration levels and the main rotor
gearboxes generated an inordinate amount of chips. At one stage BHL engineers
were changing one gearbox every week, and returning it under their innovative new
'power-by-the-hour' maintenance contract.

Aerospatiale design engineers, when they visited to help with these problems,
were horrified to learn of the use – over 200 hours in a month – to which their
products were being put and the sort of flying that was involved. They were flying
two trips to the East Shetland Basin every day, five days a week, representing up to
eleven hours per aircraft per day.

Although the gearbox chip problem persisted for many years, after a settling-in phase the Tiger started to generate enthusiastic responses from both pilots and passengers. Even during its first month of operation it met 95% of its planned commercial flight departures. Since then the Tiger has lived up to its early promise and become a firm favourite in the region.

The new helicopter went down equally well with those who had to fly it. Graham Lee, an early chief pilot on the type, considered it,

> *a marvellous aircraft, very responsive, and much more stable than the Puma J. The stabiliser and fin have a lot to do with this, but so has the autopilot. Passengers tell me that noise and vibration levels down the back are almost comparable with some fixed-wing aircraft.*
>
> *The Tiger has already proved itself immensely able, particularly in the single engine context. Our specified performance parameters have all been met; one of the most impressive being its 145 knot cruise speed.*

It was clear that the new helicopter required new training facilities. Alastair Gordon scoured the market and secured the services of a couple of simulator engineers, who had recently left one of the major manufacturers. They built him a fairly basic four-axis simulator, with no visual system. It was later upgraded with visuals but is still Category A: able to provide the most basic form of IR training.

However, over fifteen years it has formed the nucleus of a training department which is now regarded as one of the best in the world. Simulator manager Phil Carter is responsible for much of this reputation. A former pilot, Phil made it his business to find out everything he could about the system, to the stage that he can now build and replace the circuit boards if they prove troublesome. Pilots who these days make the transition from helicopter to airline flying, and who have BHL stamps in their log-books, are particularly sought after.

Phil Carter.

'You're going back in a new Bristow Tiger! You lucky swine!!' (Copyright: Tugg, 1982-2003)

Bristow Tiger.

Graham Holloway now supervises twelve Super Puma training captains, who carry out a myriad of checks on pilots flying the aircraft for BHL around the world.

When Helen Snell was taken on in October 1974 to work as a junior book-keeper, John Odlin had advised her not to take her coat off. The oil boom, in his opinion, was not likely to last more than ten years. Although Helen still works for BHL as accounts supervisor, and John Odlin has long since retired to Surrey, in a way he was right. The decade between 1975 and 1985 is still perceived as Aberdeen's heyday. There was plenty of money around and oil companies were happy to call on their helicopter support if they needed something – anything – brought from ashore. It was not unknown for an S61N to leave Aberdeen empty and return with one passenger.

Partly as a result of this level of activity, and partly because of a continuing pilot shortage, a 20% across-the-board pay rise was announced in 1980. It was almost inevitable, therefore, that when the oil price dropped a correction would have to be made. Alan Bristow had once assured his workforce that he would never make people redundant: however some pilots had to be released in 1982. In mid-1986, after Alan had retired, a further fall in the oil price to below $10 a barrel, coupled with the losses of some contracts and a few bad calls in others, led to as many as 100 redundancies being made across the board. The flight line's forty-strong ramp handling section was disbanded completely, and engineers drafted in to do their job. It was an uncertain period in the company's history: however the market eventually improved and many of them were able to be rehired.

The second AS332L avionics course at Eurocopter, Marseilles. Back row, left to right: John Matheson, French interpreter Dave Scott, Eurocopter instructor Ray Hill. Middle row: Ray Smart, Ron Patterson, Bert Forrest. Front row: Philippe Chantrel (from SFIM) and Peter Carpenter.

## CHAPTER NINE

# STRETCHING THE ENVELOPE

By the late sixties it was clear that the bulk of BHL operations were, as Jean Bristow had first suggested, involved in supporting the worldwide oil industry. Strong presence had been established in Australia, Indonesia, Iran, Malaysia, Nigeria and Trinidad, with smaller exploration contracts established almost everywhere else outside the Soviet Union and the USA.

Further contracts were secured in the Philippines and Burma, India and Pakistan. In 1972, while in Pakistan, Bryan Shaw managed to get himself involved in its war with India. Although the BHL contract with West German company Wintershall involved offshore operations from Karachi, to obtain the final military clearances Bryan had to go to the seat of government in Islamabad. In many of these countries, at the time, helicopters were regarded as having security and military implications.

Bryan secured the clearances, returned to Karachi and booked a flight for the next day. He was staying at the Intercontinental Hotel and went to the cinema in the evening. When he came out, he noticed there were no lights and the hotel was completely blacked out. War had broken out between India and Pakistan. Seventeen air-raid alarms caused Bryan to spend the entire night running up and down the staircase, from his room on the ninth floor to the air-raid shelter in the basement, and back again. As there was no electricity, there was no lift.

In the morning, he opened his curtains to see Indian Canberra jets flashing past from bombing oil storage depots in the harbour. The smoke from the fires was so dense that it blacked out the sun. During the day it seemed like the Battle of Britain was taking place overhead and the Europeans, confined to their hotel, plotted how they might escape. One of the more extreme schemes involved commandeering a Land Rover and making a 300-mile dash for the Iranian border. As it happened this proved unnecessary as pressure brought to bear on the combatants achieved an armistice which allowed foreigners to leave.

The West African state of Nigeria provokes strong and mixed emotions from the Bristow pilots, engineers and families who have seen service there over the past

The base at Port Harcourt, Nigeria, February 1964.

forty-plus years. With its roots in Fison-Airwork, it is the longest-serving operation in BHL's history. To those who harbour reservations about the place, it may come as a surprise to discover that it was once considered a plum posting. Pilot/engineer Tommy Bayden recalls the good old days, before the horrors of the 1968-1970 civil war.

> *Nigeria was great then. We had plenty of co-operation, a low cost of living, a good social life and the wives enjoyed themselves. It was one of the most popular tours we could offer. Before the war you never saw the army, the police acted all-very-British and the place still had a touch of Empire to it. Most of that has gone now.*

At the time of the Biafran secession, BHL had eleven helicopters committed to oil support work, all technically based at Port Harcourt. Two Whirlwind 3s, four Hiller 12E4s and five Widgeons, as well as a Riley Dove and a Twin Pioneer, were semi-permanently allocated to Shell-BP, Amoseas and Mobil.

However the secession and the subsequent war changed everything. Tommy was there when it started to go badly wrong.

> *Nobody knew what was going to happen. We were on tenterhooks wondering whether it was going to peter out or turn nasty. In the end it got nasty, so we had to evacuate – many of our Nigerian employees fled. The order came in the middle of a crew change – we were sent to a rig somewhere and told to stay put.*

*We managed to get a suitcase of stuff each, but all the rest of our belongings were in the bungalows and there it stayed. There was a 48-hour truce to evacuate all the expats who, once the war started, were in very real danger. We were ferrying them from the rigs, linking them up with their families and their dogs and cats, and then flying them to Fernando Po.*

Tommy and the rest of the Bristow men stayed behind and found themselves facing the same sort of dilemma that would be repeated in Iran twelve years later: how to stay out of someone else's fight without making them more trigger-happy than they already were.

*The Biafrans wanted to use us to recce the coast, looking for Federal ships that had been bombarding them in Port Harcourt. We just said no. There wasn't much they could do but they made it plain they didn't like us. The British definitely weren't popular: our government was helping the Federals up in Lagos and we were at the other, rebel end of the country. They were all pointing the finger at us, saying our government was helping their enemies. Things were looking slightly dangerous but, fortunately, they were very fair in allowing us to move out without hostages being taken. I must admit it was all quite exciting – it certainly got the adrenaline going.*

However, not all the dangers in the area came from the warring Nigerian factions, as pilot Peter Gray found out for himself. He was stationed in the country when the war broke out and was detailed to fly a Whirlwind back to Redhill. Getting out of Nigeria proved not to be too difficult and it seemed that the only problem facing Peter and his crew, as they flew along the West African coast, would be the forecast strong headwinds and torrential rain. But as he flew over the small Portuguese colony of Guinea – now Guinea-Bissau – en route to The Gambia, he was given a rude awakening.

*We were joined by a DC3 with its wheels and flaps down. It stayed with us so I waved, dismissing it as a curious observer. We pressed on regardless but soon became aware of a number of huge splashes in the swamp below and ahead of us, accompanied by loud thumps. Seconds later, a Fiat jet fighter screamed around in front of us, dropping his wheels and flaps.*

*I realised that it had been firing at us. It started to circle so I turned and kept inside its orbits, gaining height all the time, and put out a Mayday. Despite a great deal of radio traffic – all of it in rapid Portuguese – there was no reply. The fighter pilot realised he was not going to catch us in his sights again so he flew away behind us. I set course again, increased to max power and continued to put out Maydays, at the same time searching over my shoulder for the jet. We had only a few more miles to go to the border.*

*By now, the jet had reappeared and my radio calls were being answered in English. I was ordered to turn around and fly to Bissau, the capital of Guinea, which lay behind us. I said that I was on an international flight from Freetown to The Gambia, which was true, and that I didn't think I'd have enough fuel to make Bissau – which wasn't. But they weren't having any of it. Shortly afterwards an Alouette arrived, took station on us just outside the disc and pointed a large machine gun at us. I took the hint.*

Alan Bristow managed to secure the release of Peter Grey's crew from Portuguese Guinea.

Peter had been unlucky enough to fly across one of the vicious little bush wars that were plaguing Africa at the time. Portuguese Guinea was constantly under attack by Nationalist guerrillas, whose supplies arrived mostly by large Russian helicopters that happened to be painted grey. While the Portuguese often picked these up on radar, they had never managed to intercept one. When Peter's Whirlwind, in its grey Bristow livery, innocently flew into their airspace, the Portuguese must have thought that they had finally hit the jackpot. The Whirlwind had been picked up on the radar and the only available aircraft, the DC3, was detailed to keep it in sight until a jet could be scrambled.

The Portuguese authorities were polite but firm. Over glasses of Johnny Walker Black Label, an Air Force officer informed the aircrew in fluent English that, although it was obvious that the mistake was all on his part, there was no question of them being released immediately. There followed days of interrogation, firstly in a fourth-rate hotel but later in prison. The conditions, of course, were no better than anyone might expect.

Back at Redhill, however, things were beginning to happen. The BUA representative in the Gambia informed Redhill that the helicopter had not arrived. He added that it had probably been detained over Portuguese Guinea, which was a not-unusual occurrence. The Foreign Office was contacted and they in turn contacted the Portuguese Embassy – which denied all knowledge of the matter.

By now, Alan Bristow was extremely angry and bluntly informed the Portuguese authorities that he knew full well they were illegally holding his personnel and one of his aircraft in Guinea. If they were not released forthwith, he would hold a press conference and inform the world of what, precisely, he thought of the role of the

Portuguese in West Africa. Whether that was the catalyst or not, that same day, twenty-six days after they were first intercepted, the Bristow men were freed. They were escorted to the border by the Alouette and the jet, and allowed to continue their flight home.

Bristow retained a skeleton presence in Lagos and the mid-western town of Warri during the war – Terry Young recalls spending a lot of his time pushing a Jet Ranger in and out of bushes to escape rocket attacks – and Bob Roffe was posted there as manager in October 1970. He recalls: 'Between 1970 and 1975, Nigeria wasn't a popular spot and we had a high staff turnover. We were involved in a lot of work elsewhere in the world and options for the lads; Iran, the Far East, Trinidad and so on, were very tempting. I don't think many people did more than a two-year stint in Nigeria at this time.'

Jim Macaskill was the last Bristow man out. In fact he went missing for several days and his colleagues were concerned. When he finally surfaced in Lagos, he said he was late because he had to inhibit the engines on all the aircraft.

After the war many of the local BHL employees, who had been in danger of persecution during the hostilities, returned from the bush and started working for the company again. Stalwarts such as radio technician Monday Ogeni and engineering assistant Vitus Ibe stayed for as many as thirty years and several Nigerians later qualified as pilots and engineers.

HRH the Duke of Edinburgh visits Kanyang, Nigeria, 1979.

In his capacity as manager, Bob Roffe sometimes had to deal with the more unpleasant side of life in the country. One of his more onerous tasks was handling what seemed like an endless stream of court cases. In the five years he was there it seemed there was never a time when he didn't have one hanging round his neck – Bristow being sued by landlords, sued for vehicle damage, sued for wrongful dismissal and so on.

Two or three employees even experienced spells in jail. In 1974 an engineer was sentenced to ten years for possession of cannabis. He served a year in the notorious Kiri-Kiri prison before being released and deported.

Whether it was a result of the heat, or the humidity, or of simply trying to remain sane in insane situations, life in Nigeria honed a pilot's sense of the ludicrous to a fine edge. Bill Farnell was a natural helicopter driver who was said to have found his spiritual home in Nigeria. It was he who would come wandering over to his helicopter on the arm of a crewman, tapping away with a white stick and his eyes obscured by sunglasses. As he climbed into the cockpit his passengers suddenly remembered other appointments. Or perhaps he'd hand one of his passengers the flight manual, smile disarmingly and say, 'I'm only up to page five – could you call out the instructions from page six onwards?'

Bill gave new life to a number of old aviation japes. On one occasion in a survey camp, he had to wait a while to pick up two passengers. To kill time he got into the back of the aircraft and started reading a book. Soon afterwards the passengers turned up, spotted Bill and asked him what time the pilot would arrive. Keeping a perfectly straight face he replied, 'I don't know. We were supposed to go at four and it's four thirty now.' He returned to his book, but a short while later announced, 'to hell with this – the damned fellow isn't going to turn up! I'm sure I can fly this thing.' With that he got into the pilot's seat and started the engine – as his passengers dived out of the helicopter and ran off in all directions. It took Bill twenty minutes to catch them and another ten to persuade them that he was indeed the real pilot.

While a posting to Nigeria had its faults, other countries never made anything but the best of impressions on Bristow men if they were appointed there, often with their families. From the company's arrival in 1957, right up to the start of the revolution of 1978, Iran was popular with everyone who lived and worked there. Bill Petrie, who was working on the piston-engined Whirlwinds with Alan Bristow from the very beginning, recalls it with special affection.

*It was a spectacular country, but the terrain presented a lot of problems for helicopters. We were doing things with the old Whirlwinds that people today would say were impossible. But we set rigid safety procedures, a high standard of maintenance, and ran a safe operation.*

*The cost of living was low, which gave you the opportunity to really see the country. I ate Iranian food, picked up a little Farsi and got to know some of the people. Returning there over a period of time helped me to see what sort of changes the Shah was making. They really were quite dramatic in things like education, health, agriculture. Whatever else he might have done, the Shah turned Iran into a modern country.*

A long-nose Whirlwind (EP-HAK) in the Zagros mountains, December 1966. One of the signatures on the back of the photograph is Gerhardt Trösch.

Offshore Lavan Island, July 1975. (Photo John Black)

Bell 212 with magnetic anomaly detector, Prakla, Iran.

If Bill liked the Iranians they, in turn, held him in affection and respect. In part, this sprang from his reputation as a fearless scorpion handler.

*We had an Iranian who claimed to be a scorpion handler and, sure enough, he'd let these things run all over him with obvious impunity. One day he brought along a big, white scorpion – supposedly the most deadly – in a box. I was curious to see how he did it, so I spied on him from my tent. He trapped the scorpion with a forked stick and then just snipped the sting out of its tail with a pair of scissors. Next, he came over to where I was working, with this scorpion running around his hand and up his sleeve. I said to him,*
*'They're very dangerous these things, aren't they?'*
*'Oh yes! Touch them and they'll kill you!'*
*Despite his obvious reluctance I took it from him. The Iranians couldn't believe that a white man would take such a risk. Alan Green was watching as well, and he couldn't believe it either – he thought I'd gone bananas! I played around with it a bit and then gave it back. He never did his scorpion trick again: he knew he'd been rumbled.*

Bill Farnell worked in Iran too. Always the practical joker, he caught Jean Dennel out on several occasions so Jean decided to get his own back. He knew that Bill's post-flight routine invariably involved a shower and a change of clothes, so he hid in the wardrobe in his room. When Bill opened it, he found Jean slumped with a rope around his neck – eyes fixed and tongue lolling. Apparently Bill's reaction made up for all the times when Jean had been the butt of his jokes.

The Iranian standard of living was high and, once the expats learned the art of haggling, their BHL salaries went a lot further. For many years Erica Barnett, wife of engineer Bill, was on hand to act as unofficial 'auntie' to any uncertain newcomers. The social life was good and living conditions were comfortable. Bob Roffe identified another factor.

> *Happiness overseas is a happy wife. If she wasn't content, then a guy would never be able to settle, so we'd do our best to help her fit in. There was a decent social life, with clubs and functions to help her pass the time when her husband was away. She'd manage to save a bit of money so she would be happy to stay. It was in the company's interest as well to keep her happy, as the costs of moving on from a two-year appointment are very high. We'd only view it as a success if someone stayed for a minimum of four years: then it was better for him and better for the company.*

Iran grew to become one of the company's biggest operations, and also one of its most diverse. There was mountain flying, offshore operations and the training school in Tehran. When in late 1978 resistance to the Shah's regime began to come into the open, many of the Bristow people could not – or did not – want to believe that it was all coming to an end. As the violence escalated, however, the reality of the

B212s, Prakla, Iran.

Tommy Bayden keeping up the fluid intake in Oman, 1981. A Dubai detachment flew survey missions for Shell in the north of the country.

situation became increasingly obvious. The story of Bristow's final escape is related in the next chapter but little has been recorded of the personal problems which confronted some men, in their attempts to leave the beleaguered country.

German pilot Horst Neu was faced with the problem of how to get large amounts of money out of the country, before it could be appropriated by the revolutionary government.

*In January 1979 I was sitting on a million rials! It was all in the bank and I knew that trying to get it out would be a hell of a job: everything was in absolute chaos. Freddy Ziegler and I went down to the bank and parked there overnight. We had to stay in the car because there was a 2200 to 0500 curfew, but to have any chance of success at the bank you had to be there early. People started queuing up at 0600 for when it opened at 0800.*

*Fat chance. Nobody was taking any notice of the curfew and the queue was all along the main road. I couldn't believe it! So we joined the queue. We managed to get inside the bank and get the paperwork sorted out. We were approaching the cashier to receive our money when he shouted, 'one o'clock!' and the shutters came down for the whole day. We had to come back the next morning and take another number. We slept out for another two nights with the same result. We didn't get all our money from the bank, though. Not ever.*

Oil rig fires, Dubai 1974. (Photo Tony Fellows)

Eventually, Horst resorted to the black market. He managed to get some of his money out but still has a sizeable stake gathering dust in an Iranian bank. On reflection, he considers himself lucky to have escaped intact:

> When the Iranians opened up the armouries in the army barracks they grabbed everything they could lay their hands on. They took off in a convoy of vehicles – private cars, military trucks – and came past our place shooting into the air and screaming. They headed west and opened up the prisons, letting everyone out. The following day the papers showed pictures of how people were actually treated in those prisons, just to show us that what we'd always suspected was true – that the Shah, despite having made some positive changes within Iran, was a tyrant.

Although working in other Middle Eastern countries promised better stability, the growing confidence and prosperity of many of them led them to decide they would be better off running a greater proportion of their own commerce. The Abu Dhabi (ex-Das Island) operation came to an end in 1975, when it was nationalised. In this case, in contrast to the handover of many overseas operations which were achieved by training up local people over a number of years, this was not handled particularly well by the government; at one point, to register a protest, BHL refused to fly. However Chris Fry eventually managed to negotiate 'quite a fair' demobilisation package over two months, which allowed base manager John Willis and his team to recover most of their costs.

Oman, Army labourers were available for assistance in loading and refuelling.

Oman. The local briefing file says, 'Station 1 – Upper Tibat. Prepared landing area is on ridge, has pronounced rearward slope and is very limited, with 2-3ft of safe ground either side of front and rear wheels. The drop-off either side is 1,500ft to sea level. It is essential that a crewman is carried'.

On the other hand BHL had built up a strong relationship in nearby Dubai, flying up to three Bell 212s and a solitary B206 for the Dubai Petroleum Co. over many years. It also maintained the helicopters owned by the state's Police Air Wing – a service that also provided valuable links to the ruler's son, Sheikh Mohammed. These stood the company in good stead when the time came to evacuate the Iranian operation in 1979, when local air traffic control turned a blind eye to Iranian demands for the fleeing helicopters and their crews to be apprehended.

Although the police contract continues into the 21st century, similar pressure to nationalise the Dubai oil support contract built during the early eighties. The operation was nationalised in mid-1984.

In 1981 word started spreading that the Malaysian Prime Minister, Dr Mahatir Mohammed, wanted to see a national helicopter company created. Having learned hard lessons in the Persian Gulf, BHL management decided to take the bull by the horns. It approached the government and proposed that it buy all BHL assets, by now including more than a dozen helicopters and three fixed-wing aircraft, and enter into a management contract. Bristow would train Malaysian pilots and engineers and hand them over to a new company, Malaysian Helicopter Services. The deal, which was at first resisted, was completed in February 1983 and a management contract, scheduled to last five years or so, continued to the end of the nineties when the last expatriate engineer left.

From the early eighties the company felt that the People's Republic of China – or more specifically the South China Sea off Hong Kong – presented a strong potential market. Regional director Chris Fry made contact with officials of the country's civil aviation administration but felt that, in those early days at least, they were making unreasonable demands of BHL. At about the same time BP was drilling sixteen dry wells so, at one point, Chris was on the point of giving up. Since BHL also won the Falkland Islands military support contract at about the same time, the resources were needed elsewhere.

In early 1984, however, Chris had a call from the Japanese Nissho-Iwai trading house in London, which said it had an opening for helicopters to operate in China. He agreed to meet them; still working on the hunch that the market was worth cultivating.

In Hong Kong he was introduced to representatives from the China Ocean Helicopter Corporation. Former partner PHI had decided to withdraw its single Bell 214ST and COHC, conscious of its limited experience at the time, needed to inject extra credibility with the oil companies. Chris quickly negotiated a draft agreement and the two companies made a joint bid to fly two Super Pumas and a Puma J from Xili Heliport in Shenzen – just over the then border with the New Territories – to rigs 140 miles out to sea. The bid succeeded and operations commenced in August 1984. The Japanese Huanan Oil Development Co., together with a consortium of Agip, Chevron and Texaco, soon struck copious quantities of oil – in exactly the

Malaysian Helicopter Services Sdn Bhd was formed in February 1983. Alan Bristow, Chris Fry, Bryan Collins and solicitor Andrew Muriel. (Photo Malcolm Pendrill)

same area where BP had earlier drilled all those dry holes. The partners still devote up to ten Super Pumas to the operation.

As well as oil support duties, winter typhoon evacuations play a regular part of the helicopter crews' duties. However the different rigs depend on a variety of weather reports and, such is their inconsistency, that one crew may find itself evacuating one group from one rig while another, simultaneously, is taking another one back. They also winch ship pilots down to the decks of the tankers, to guide them to mooring buoys where they can hook up to the oil pipeline. An average of thirty of these evolutions every month make it, still, the largest public transport winching operation in the world.

In 1979 Alan Bristow, after strong lobbying from some senior oil company figures, decided to enter the offshore business in the Gulf of Mexico. A small Texas-based helicopter company – Offshore Helicopters Inc. – was purchased, along with a dockside service base at Sabine Pass in East Texas.

Bristow Offshore Helicopters Inc., initially run by Chuck Bond, was established to compete with US operators that provided a 'day-VMC' only service, using mainly small single-engined helicopters, over the relatively benign waters of the Gulf. BOHI offered the oil companies a twenty-four-hour IFR service using twins. However, although everyone took advantage of it during the trials – and the roughnecks loved it because it guaranteed a regular return 'to the beach' – the cost of providing the service proved too high for the local oil company managers, with their tight budgets and a tradition of preferring smaller helicopters.

BOHI also had problems with its S76s. Paralleling their introduction to the North Sea operation, their early Allison engines suffered considerable teething problems. Sikorsky was put under severe pressure to resolve them and, in an effort to help, dispatched its own factory demonstrator to serve, free-of-charge, as a back-up machine. By now Chuck Bond had handed over to John Odlin, who was supported by Ian Clark as operations manager. Dick Davidson, followed by Derek Cook and Sandy Ogilvie, supported them on the engineering side.

It soon became obvious that the customers were not going to pay for a guaranteed service. The American venture was not going to be a commercial success so, at the end of 1981, Alan closed it down. It was an expensive failure. BOHI had been run as a full US operation, under American ownership. One board member was the author James Clavell, a former schoolmate and life-long friend of Alan Bristow.

Although the operation's failure had nothing to do with him, John Odlin was disappointed. He went back to Aberdeen for a few months as – as he puts it – an over-qualified line pilot, before taking on a commercial position at Redhill.

In 1984, for the first time since Alan Bristow's Air Whaling days, Bristow Helicopters returned to the Antarctic. Two Bell Jet Rangers (G-AVIG and G-AWMK) were flown onboard Royal Research Ship *Bransfield* in Southampton Water in October. Three pilots and two engineers (Dave Mallock, John Shaw, Andrew Rice, Dave Simpson and Eddie Lawrenson), then flew down to Cape Town to join the ship there, for a voyage to resupply the bases of the British Antarctic Survey (BAS).

Bell 206 in RRS *Bransfield*, 1984.

The ship arrived at Halley Base in mid-December, and moored to the ice shelf. Several flights were made but the bulk of the base resupply was done by snow-cat and the helicopter team worked alongside the ship's crew unloading on to the ice. This continued twenty-four hours a day, as the sun circled the horizon without setting. The ship then continued south and spent the New Year beset in the pack-ice. A couple of survey flights were flown but, recalls Andrew, most of the time was spent in the bar.

On 4 January, the ship became stuck in the ice once again and the helicopters were used to set up a fuel depot for the BAS Twin Otters to use later. Unfortunately, on 5 January, G-AVIG crashed onto the ice shelf while en-route back to the ship, and was totally destroyed. At the time MK was carrying a load to the depot and landed to pick up the uninjured pilot and passengers. Without a second aircraft, which was required for mutual SAR, operations had to stop. The following day the sea-ice broke up and the ship was able to get alongside the main ice shelf and offload the rest of the fuel by snow-cat.

*The ship continued its task, with only an occasional local flight in the area. We were able to deliver some gifts to the Soviet supply ship Kapitan Mishevski for the Russian new year before setting off, on 18 January, towards Montevideo to crew-change the BAS personnel. While in Uruguay a new 206, G-BLPL, was loaded on board with Bob Innes, and the Bransfield once again headed south.*

During March several flights were made on the east side of the Antarctic Peninsula, mainly to carry underslung loads for a depot on Spaatz Island. G–BLPL was deployed to the UK base at Rothera on 18 March and flew some survey flights for a proposed base airstrip. A geology recce was also made to Pourquoi Pas Island, during which the aircraft briefly landed on a 500ft-high iceberg. At the end of March the *Bransfield* turned north and headed for the Falkland Islands. The helicopter team left the ship in Stanley and flew back to the UK in an RAF C130.

Despite the odd setback, however, the 1970s and early '80s were a period of rapid international growth. Many contracts were won and some were lost, but none required disestablishing quite so dramatically as the company's substantial presence in Iran, in 1979. The evacuation operation it involved would later be seen as one of its proudest moments.

CHAPTER TEN

# SANDSTORM OVER THE GULF

Shortly before 0700 on Friday 9 March 1979, Pym White keyed the HF transmitter in his small office at Sharjah Airport, Dubai. His message – 'We have strong sandstorms this morning, exactly as forecast yesterday' – set in motion one of the most audacious escapes in the history of civil aviation.

Within minutes of its transmission, five B212 helicopters and their crews lifted off from under the eyes and guns of local revolutionary committees and were on their way to safety out of post-revolutionary Iran. Two more, delayed by a communications hiccup, nearly did not make it.

Bristow's decision to pull out of the country, thus severing a link which had been first forged in 1957, was not taken lightly. Even as the political situation was deteriorating, and normal operations becoming impractical, it was still felt that something could be salvaged from the mess. When the last members of staff had left the Iranian Helicopters Aviation Co.'s Tehran office, two weeks earlier, it was felt that the remaining Iranian operations – at Kharg Island, Gach Saran and Lavan – could continue even if they had to be directed from Dubai. The fact of the matter, however, was that IHAC was no longer being paid by its customers and, consequently, for six months BHL had not been paid.

There had been intermittent disturbances in outlying towns and villages throughout Iran from April 1978, but it was not until 8 September, when fierce rioting broke out on the streets of Tehran, that the revolution really began. On that day the Shah sacked his civilian government, introduced martial law, and set a 2100-0500 curfew on city streets.

Ten days later, following a week of bombings in restaurants and an explosion in an Abadan cinema – causing considerable loss of life – regional director Chris Fry put out a warning advising BHL personnel to stay away. Pilot Bruce Fleming and his family had already had a narrow escape, when the restaurant in which they were eating was damaged by a rebel bomb.

From the imposition of the curfew there were daily riots in Tehran, particularly in the downtown banking area close to the BHL office. At night troops met passive

How the *Daily Express* reported the escape.

resistance from crowds of Iranians shouting defiance from the rooftops. Cars were overturned and burned, with columns of smoke visible for miles around.

Engineering director Bill Petrie found that visiting his scattered operations was becoming difficult. A series of lightning strikes by various Iran Air departments meant that on one day there might be no ticket clerks; the next no baggage handlers and the next no pilots. The curfew made travelling difficult and the only way he could visit Gach Saran, normally a one-and-a-half hour flight, was by driving 700 miles over rough roads, then spending a night at Esfahan and a second at Shiraz, and flying the rest of the way by helicopter.

When Iranian customs went on strike Chris Fry, anxious to keep BHL machines flying, took to bringing vital aircraft spares in his luggage whenever he visited from the UK. Notwithstanding the strike, he was invariably stopped by customs but always managed to bluff his way through.

From the rooftop of Pym White's house in the suburbs, visiting regional flying superintendent John Cameron could hear the surge of crowds massing in the heart

Departing Zagros. (Photo John Black)

of the city. From about 2100 the chanting started – 'Allah Akbar, Allah el Allah, Allah, Allah' – and would be taken up until it spread across the entire city. Mains power would be switched off and the house plunged into darkness.

There would be sporadic machine-gun fire. White's rooftop proved a useful vantage point and, when the rioting became especially fierce, wives would phone the office with directions as how to avoid the hot-spots while trying to get home.

During the weekend of 4 and 5 November, the troubles reached a new peak when university students rioted and troops opened fire. On 6 November, the Shah made his first (and last) broadcast to the nation, declaring that the curfew and martial law were merely temporary measures.

At Redhill, Chris Fry advised Alan Bristow that the time had come for BHL families to be brought home. Most of them were only too glad to accept his recommendation, as life in Tehran was becoming intolerable. Schools and banks were closed; fresh food was in short supply and petrol scarce.

A shortage in jet fuel meant a reduction in flying hours and a halt to charter flights made crew rotation almost impossible. At Lavan, a small refinery on an island in the south of Iran, the only people not on strike were IHAC employees. Although relations with their local labourers remained friendly, demonstrations and a degree of hostility from its oil company customers, Lapco and Iminoco, was directed at all expatriates – especially Americans, so US pilot Andy Cairns had to maintain a particularly low profile. Trucks at the heliport would develop sudden flat tyres and strikers at the jetty would chant 'foreigners go home'.

As the heliport provided the only means of ferrying casualties to hospital, and food to the security guards on the strike-bound oil platforms, strike leaders allowed the flying to continue. In his December report Lavan chief pilot Yves Le Roy was stoical. 'When will we see a charter? Latest news – the airports are closed. Happy New Year?'

At Bandar Pahlavi, on the Caspian Sea to the north-west of Tehran, a one-Bell 206 Jet Ranger operation was taken off its forestry contract. Pilot Dick Collishaw returned to the UK while engineer Alan Storey, married to an Iranian girl, stayed on to complete a maintenance check on the helicopter. The area close to Galeh Morghi, the military airfield at Tehran where another Jet Ranger was based, became increasingly dangerous. Rather than risk driving through it, pilot Don Macdonald would first drive to Mehrabad International Airport and then fly to Galeh Morghi, in another helicopter that was kept there especially for the purpose. It was a two-mile flight.

Fuel became increasingly scarce. Even the fuel in the helicopters' tanks was not safe: on several occasions crews would arrive in the morning to discover they had been drained – almost certainly for cooking or heating purposes in that poverty-stricken area.

The chief pilot at Kharg Island, Stuart Clegg, cut December flying hours by two-thirds. Towards the end of the month all IPAC (Iran Pan-American Oil Company) fields stopped production and Clegg reduced his commitment by one aircraft. Later that month, after an incident in Ahwaz in which a senior American was shot dead, expatriate members of some companies began to receive live bullets in the mail.

Bell 212. (Photo John Black)

At Gach Saran an oil pipeline was sabotaged and, on Christmas Day, local workers walked out. On 30 December a B212 (EP-HBM) and its crew arrived from the newly-evacuated Baraghan Oil Centre, a small offshore operation to the south. On New Year's Eve, rioting broke out in the nearby village and chief pilot John Black ordered all BHL personnel to move to the nearby Foster-Wheeler camp.

Back in Tehran, the BHL expatriates stayed on friendly terms with their Iranian colleagues. IHAC managers, however, were nervous and uncertain as to where their loyalties lay. If rioting became fierce they would take the Shah's picture down from the wall and replace it with that of the Ayatollah Khomeini. When things calmed down, the Shah's would return. To be on the safe side, local drivers would carry photographs of both and soon even the expats followed suit.

In January, the British school delayed its reopening and long queues started to build at petrol stations. Towards the end of the month Mehrabad Airport took to closing, without warning, for long periods: making visits to the other operations almost impossible. Telephone communications between Tehran and Redhill became increasingly difficult.

Back in Redhill, John Cameron telexed authorities in Bahrain, Kuwait and Dubai asking for permission for any IHAC aircraft leaving Iran to ferry through their respective territories.

It was decided to evacuate the remaining families. Finding seats on outbound aircraft was difficult. British Airways could not guarantee seats and other airlines were full. Alan Bristow attempted to charter an aircraft from Dubai but could not get landing or handling clearance. Eventually BA came up with enough seats for a flight home on 7 January.

John Willis.

Soon after this it began to snow heavily; adding to the discomfort. Power cuts every night, as well as most days, meant heating was sporadic. John Willis and his colleagues were struggling to keep things running and to maintain the flow of funds to the remote operations. Payment from their Iranian clients dried up. During a visit from the UK, Chris Fry managed to get £200,000 in part payment but this, relatively speaking, was a drop in the ocean.

Meanwhile, the Bandar Pahlavi Jet Ranger was in pieces, halfway through its aborted Check 2. At Gach Saran the operation was reduced to one B212 and one Jet Ranger, plus another on standby. The operation which had decamped to Foster-Wheeler, returned to Gach Saran on 26 January, leaving a single B212 in place.

One full-scale field crew change was carried out, involving a twenty-three-hour coach journey from Tehran, through Esfahan and Shiraz to Bushire. The pilots and engineers there had been waiting for several weeks. The trip took place on 16 January – the day of the Shah's abdication. They drove through the streets of one small town, 200 miles south of the capital, full of thousands of shouting Iranians.

Reaching Galeh Morghi was becoming difficult. Three B212s were now locked up there – one was in the middle of a 1,000-hour check. Pym White tried to fly eight engineers in from Mehrabad, but spent four hours lobbying various generals before being allowed to take off. The helicopters were finally flown out – by Horst Neu, Al Meier and Jim Jacobs – to Dubai, via Gach Saran and Esfahan, arriving on 31 January.

It was now time to start a move towards Sharjah Airport in Dubai, which boasted better communications with both the Iranian operation and Redhill. By early February, the company HS125 had arrived and the crews were starting the long process of shifting helicopter spare parts from the Tehran office. Over one weekend engineering manager Geoff Francis and logistics engineer Malcolm Ellis, together with a team of technicians and pilots, sorted, packed and logged scores of packages to be loaded into the jet.

As the situation deteriorated, the ways in which spares and effects found their way out of Tehran became more and more imaginative. Engineer John Beehan liberated 400kg of parts, loaded into ten suitcases marked 'personal effects'. On at least eight occasions, Geoff Francis and Peter Frean would drive full VW vans in convoy to the airport; looking for a friendly customs officer whom they could bribe with five gallons of petrol. By the time the last expat left Tehran in February, only a few large stores items remained – locked in customs by the strike.

On 6 February an attempt was made to recover the Jet Ranger which had been left behind at Bandar Pahlavi. French pilot Jean-Jacques Rollin flew two engineers there in an Alouette and returned with a large quantity of spares. The following day he and Peter Frean returned for the helicopter, en route dropping off a Royal Marine officer and NCO to salvage some Army equipment.

It was about this time that the British Embassy decided to evacuate all non-essential British expats. RAF Hercules transports began to arrive at Mehrabad. Peter Frean left his home to stay with a Dutch friend in a more peaceful part of town, taking with him tinned food, drink and the company cat – 'Dogfood'. John Willis and Geoff Francis were by now sharing John's flat to the north of Tehran.

The situation changed from day to day. A few days of peace would be followed by pitched battles in the city centre. At night the sky was etched by red tracer fire and the chanting continued: 'Allah Akbar, Allah el Allah'. IHAC staff received threats but refused to take them seriously: like many Iranians they believed that their Army would stand firm. On Saturday 10 February, however, they were proved wrong when the Army started fighting with the Air Force at a local base.

The numbers of expatriate staff at the Tehran office were gradually reduced, carefully, so as not to attract the attention of the Iranians, most of who were by now resisting every move they made. By mid-February their number had fallen to around half a dozen.

From 12 February, when the Army capitulated and Prime Minister Dr Bakhtiar resigned, remaining expats felt particularly vulnerable. The need to make a decision on a Dubai move was now urgent: the whole world had been taken aback at the speed with which the Imperial Guard – the Shah's most loyal followers – had folded. Peter Frean had by now negotiated the release of three B212s, which were needed on BHL operations elsewhere. He persuaded no less an official than the deputy prime minister – Mr Emtezan – that the aircraft were unserviceable and, with spares and engineers in Dubai, of no use to him. The aircraft, he promised, would return after servicing.

The idea of evacuating all remaining BHL operations in Iran had been broached by Redhill but no decision had yet been taken in Tehran. There, they still believed things would improve.

John Willis discussed the possibility of complete evacuation with his counterpart at the other foreign helicopter operator in Iran, Dutch company Schreiner. The idea had to be floated – if one company went independently the other would then have no chance – but the Schreiner rep's reaction was that it was too great a risk. He was running smaller aircraft – incapable of covering large distances – and knew he was much more closely observed than were his British friends. Willis took comfort in the fact that, at least, he had given them the chance.

The success rate of foreigners leaving Iran unofficially was not high, but particularly for those trying to get down from the north of the country. For BHL, with its remaining operations all in the south, it would be a relatively simple matter of hopping across the Gulf. It was obvious, though, that nothing could happen while the expats remained in Tehran.

Having obtained a clearance for the BHL HS125, Peter Frean and John Willis saw their remaining expat staff – French, German and Filippino – out of Mehrebad on 19 February. British engineers found places on an RAF Hercules, leaving the two pilots to hold the Tehran fort.

The next day John rang his secretary to say he was going out for lunch, but would be back later. He met Peter at his house and, together with Dogfood and some hand luggage, the pair left for Mehrebad. There they cleared customs and boarded the HS125 – at about the time that an IHAC manager phoned Peter's house to ask where he was. 'They've gone to the airport!' the houseboy exclaimed.

Later, comfortably ensconced at the Holiday Inn, Sharjah, John and Peter, together with Pym White, Malcolm Ellis and Geoff Francis, kept in close but cautious contact with remaining BHL operations. No decision had been made regarding their future but at least, by clearing the Tehran office, they were keeping their options open.

IHAC was refusing to allow their leased helicopters, a Jet Ranger and two Alouettes, to leave Iran. They were in a hangar at Galeh Morghi and it was obvious that there they would stay. On 23 February John Willis called Alan Bristow to discuss an evacuation plan, while the other pilots looked at the available fuel and made rough calculations.

One problem loomed large – all three operations would have to begin at precisely the same time. If one was delayed, the crews and equipment were quite likely to be taken hostage.

Gach Saran was at the time less strictly controlled than Kharg Island, although life was becoming difficult. Yves Le Roy and his colleagues on Lavan enjoyed a good relationship with their local committee due, in part, to Yves' nationality. He had also managed to smooth the path with the American-influenced oil company Lapco, which was touchy about IHAC and the Iranians. He made it clear to Willis that his luck would not hold out for ever.

From Sharjah, Geoff Francis contacted the engineers at Gach Saran, Kharg and Lavan. It was a guarded conversation – the Iranian radio engineers all spoke English. Several times pilots and engineers, unable to understand why they were not being relieved, interrupted him on air to demand to know what was going on. Geoff was put in an impossible position: he could hardly tell them that they were not being relieved because they were about to be evacuated.

Still no final decision had been made but Pym White devised a code so that, if Alan Bristow gave the order to pull out, a message could be passed over HF without giving the game away. The codeword 'Sandstorm', coined by Pym to represent the order to go ahead, was especially apt – such storms were particularly frequent at this time of year. However other phrases were more elaborate.

The message 'John Willis would like clarification on some points in your imprest account and will revert to this at 7a.m. tomorrow', indicated that the outposts should prepare their aircraft for an immediate flight out of Iran with all expatriate staff. They were to await confirmation. The timing indicated the approximate timing of the executive order. Place names were encoded as well. Any operation which, on receiving the 'sandstorm' order, was not able to comply, would reply, 'We have a sandstorm at (operation's name) as well'. This slightly ambiguous message was later responsible for some anxious moments at Gach Saran.

Back at Redhill a team of four pilots – Bob Innes, Roger Vaughan, Armand Richard and Jean-Pierre Roux Levrat – were briefed by Alan Bristow. He wanted enough pilots to be in a position to fly out every helicopter to Dubai.

Chris Fry left for Dubai on 7 March. The next day he discussed the situation with Willis and White and agreed that, if Operation Sandstorm was to go ahead, it would be best to call it for the following day – Friday 9 March. It had become a case of 'now or never', since an unexpected military coup or fresh political upheaval could jeopardise the whole plan. They also thought that, since Friday was the Muslim weekend, the military were unlikely to be at full alert and local revolutionary committees, hopefully, would be at prayer.

At Redhill plans were put in place to charter a Boeing 747 and Super Guppy freighter, which would be used to fly out all the helicopters when they arrived in Dubai. Bill Petrie had the unenviable task of organising this, without knowing when or where, if at all, the helicopters would arrive from Iran.

Alan Bristow asked aviation lawyer Peter Martin to arrange UK registration for the Iranian-registered helicopters, to be applied as soon as they arrived at their destinations. Peter made this possible by identifying an obscure paragraph in the Air Navigation Order. Passport numbers of everyone involved were collected so that, in an emergency, British embassies along the route could be alerted.

On 6 March a B212 (EP-HCC) flew to Lavan on a routine crew change from Gach Saran. In order to remove more valuable spares, it was arranged that the helicopter would develop spurious engine problems. Pilot Jacques Villeneuve was, to all intents and purposes, expected to return to Gach Saran. However for the benefit of any Iranian eavesdroppers, its No.2 engine failed at Lavan. In fact it developed a different unserviceability – one of its skids was damaged by a drum while refuelling at the offshore Lapco Flow Station.

The next day Innes, Richard and Yves Le Roy flew to the Flow Station and from there to Lavan. The B212 returning from Lapco took pilot Jerry Lawrence and engineer Mike Bairstow, together with the remaining spares from Lavan and those brought from Gach Saran by EP-HCC.

On 8 March Pym White contacted the operations to find out, by careful innuendo, their favoured time for an evacuation – there was unfortunately no code that meant, 'standby to standby'. Gach Saran was, by now, under the most pressure from armed guards; as well as being the furthest away from safety. It had to be John Black who called the tune. Pym understood John to say that the morning would suit him best. As it turned out, the need for circumlocution then led to confusion at the outpost the next day.

That evening Alan Bristow, briefed by Chris Fry, decided that the time was right to order the evacuation – at 0700 the next day.

The helicopters were to fly from Kharg and Lavan to Bahrain, where they would be met by Roger Vaughan. Don Macdonald would be in Kuwait to await the arrival of John Black and Guy Causse – the Gach aircraft lacked the range to fly straight to Bahrain. The helicopters would then be flown to Sharjah for onward freighting back to the UK.

Dinner at the Holiday Inn that evening was a tense affair. Chris Fry, John Willis, Pym White and Geoff Francis were well aware that, now they had Alan Bristow's go-ahead, much of the responsibility lay on their shoulders.

After a restless night, Chris woke early to see Pym striding across to the hangar. Geoff was already there. Neither had been able to bear the suspense.

Stuart Clegg was on the radio. 'Sharjah, this is Kharg'. It was fifteen minutes earlier than the agreed time. Stuart was expecting passengers to arrive for an early flight to Sea Island and was anxious to be off before they arrived. However Pym could not give one the go-ahead without the others.

Soon Yves Le Roy came on air, ready to go. At this stage they thought they were just waiting for John Black at Gach Saran but, unknown to them, there was a fourth helicopter standing by.

One of the Gach Saran's B212s was at Foster-Wheeler. When pilot Sam Blair called in, Pym guessed that John Black was also ready to leave. However Gach Saran was not yet in contact.

No harm, thought Pym, could come from giving the go-ahead a few minutes early. 'We have strong sandstorms exactly as forecast yesterday. We will keep transmissions to a minimum but listen out on this frequency and we will talk to you later.' 'Roger', said Foster-Wheeler. 'Roger', said Kharg. 'Roger', said Lavan.

A full thirty-two minutes after the deadline passed, a plaintive voice came on the HF. 'Do you have a message for us? We are all ears.' To his horror, Pym recognised John Black's voice. 'John, is that you?' 'Yes, we are all ears.' The one operation that faced the most risk hadn't heard the Sandstorm message. Trying to suppress his shock and frustration, Pym passed it again. 'Roger', said Gach Saran.

Five minutes after receiving the word, pilot Stuart Clegg and engineer Dixie Newton in EP-HBL, together with Andy Cairns and Joe Siatong in BI, were on their way from Kharg across the Gulf to Bahrain – 180 miles away. To cover their tracks they had left the hangar and office doors open: a solitary guard wished them 'good morning' and continued to eat berries from a tree. They took off in different directions, so as not to alert anti-aircraft artillery crews who were used to seeing only singletons.

With only VHF on board, they had no way of knowing that, at the time, John Black at Gach Saran had not received the go-ahead. The Kharg radio operator, who arrived at work shortly after the helicopters had taken off, lost no time in flashing messages to Gach Saran and Tehran in a bid to discover their whereabouts.

Stuart and Andy flew low-level, maintaining radio silence, along standard routes as far as they could to avoid alerting radar. Visibility was poor and, for most of the journey, they couldn't see each other. BI had long-range tanks but, when BL's fuel ran low, Stuart had to bring it to the hover while Dixie Newton refuelled it manually, from drums in the cabin.

Two hours later the pair arrived in Bahrain and Roger Vaughan, waiting at the airport, was able to pass on the good news to Sharjah. The Iranian registrations were immediately replaced with new British ones.

The three Lavan B212s – EP-HBQ, CA and CC, newly arrived from Gach Saran – had only 140 miles to fly to Dubai. Although they had been working there, without relief, for over three months, Yves Le Roy in particular was sad to leave. As a Frenchman he had built particularly good relations with the local community and was a well-liked figure.

On the morning of 9 March, Le Roy and Villeneuve were ready to go. They had decided that, since five aircraft taking off at once would arouse immediate suspicion – the base was in close proximity to Kish radar and a fighter base – they would abandon the two Alouettes as decoys. Two Bell 212s (CA and BQ) could be flown out immediately, ostensibly on a training mission, but CC was to be delayed while its spurious engine fault could be investigated. Bob Innes judged that the damaged skid would hold together for this one flight.

Villeneuve and Armand Richard took off in CA on their training sortie, followed by Le Roy in BQ. They flew out to the Iminoco platform at normal height, for the benefit of radar, then bypassed it and flew on to Dubai. They listened out for CC on HF.

Meanwhile Bob Innes was putting his Bell through a complex series of mock ground runs: some of the local labourers had been on the operation for thirteen years and there wasn't much they didn't know about B212 operations. Final checks were made, Bob began a hover check and Martin Boardley told the chief labourer that they wanted to do an hour's air test to the north of the island. 'Get the boys out and have a cup of tea. We'll see you later.'

At 0900 they took off and flew to pick up engineers Ian Ostler and Gerry Geronimo, who had driven into the desert with their luggage to avoid the obvious impression it would have given, had they put it in the helicopter. They then set off for the Gulf.

Le Roy and Boardley, unhappy to be leaving under these circumstances, managed to thank the Lavan labourers for their loyalty. Boardley left references for them on his desk, should they come across the Gulf looking for work. Le Roy borrowed 300,000 rials from Lapco, so that he could pay them up to date. This was seen as fair enough, since Lapco had for some time been underpaying local suppliers.

The weather was bad during the flight: sandstorms (real ones) on land and 25-knot winds, thunderstorms and low visibility at sea. Although they had planned to make for Bahrain, the presence of the air defence radar on Kish also convinced Innes that

Dubai was the safer bet. Low on fuel, they took on 1,000lb of Jet A1 at Fateh and then made for Dubai, where Le Roy and Villeneuve – and Pym White – were waiting for them.

Safe and sound by midday on the 9th, the crews were also downcast. They were convinced that, having left before the Gach Saran men were able to, they were certain to have been captured. They had been less than 200 miles from Kuwait and should have arrived by now.

When Pym White had passed the 'imprest' message on 7 March, he unwittingly set John Black a problem. Although he could expect the 'sandstorm' message at 0700, he had a revenue flight scheduled for 1100. He wanted to delay the departures until after that when, with his labourers off to lunch, they would attract far less attention. Meanwhile Terry and Margaret Watts and Andy Harding would drive the twenty miles to the Foster-Wheeler outpost, with their luggage, and wait to be picked up.

John thought he had made his preference clear to Pym White so, when he received the 'sandstorm' message, he was mortified. He became even more worried when, thirty minutes later, he began to receive calls from the radio operator at Kharg, asking if he had seen their helicopters. He reassured him that they were on their way to Gach Saran but the man's suspicions were definitely aroused. John decided they would have to leave anyway.

He convinced the airport manager that he should get airborne to act as a VHF relay with the 'inbound' Kharg helicopters. He would then leave to carry out the scheduled flight. He sent the ground party off to Foster-Wheeler leaving all personal effects in the Staff House to avoid any suspicion of an evacuation, and with engineer Mike Bardos, loaded CB with toolboxes and documents. Just as they were starting up, the airport manager appeared and indicated that he wanted to go up with them. Fortunately John was able to convince him that this was not possible.

At 1000, Black and Bardos got airborne in CB and started to send spurious position reports to the radio operators at both Kharg and Gach Saran, in an effort to persuade them that they were searching for the 'missing' aircraft. Instead they flew, via a circuitous route, to Foster-Wheeler to pick up the ground party. They hadn't arrived but Guy Causse and Sam Blair were waiting in BU. Trying to prolong the deception, BU took off and waited out of sight, while John waited another ten minutes for the VW van to arrive. The group then loaded up and took off, leaving the van doors open and the engine running.

The pair soon joined up and flew to the coast, staying low and clear of any human activity. John sent a final 'position report' to Kharg, saying he had found one of the 'missing' helicopters on a beach close to Bushire and was landing to investigate. He would, he told them, report in ten minutes. In fact, prior to continuing over the sea to Kuwait, they landed on the beach to refuel from the drum each carried.

Instead, with a steady easterly wind and reducing visibility, they dashed for the sea – low-level, to avoid the Abadan radar. As they skimmed the wave-tops close to an Iraqi oil terminal, a huge tanker loomed out of the murk ahead of them. Sweeping along the length of its hull they could see men on deck, looking down at them.

Kuwait radar was out of action and John was unable to contact them until he was ten miles out. Using only his abbreviated call-sign, rather than the incriminating Iranian identifier, he called for an emergency diversion – thus ensuring permission to land.

The pair flew on until they came abeam an island which John knew belonged to Kuwait. After a short water crossing they found the airport and landed at 1230.

When word of the Gach Saran crews' escape reached Sharjah, Geoff Francis rushed out of the radio room towards his dispirited colleagues. 'They've made it – they've made it!' Bob Innes all but collapsed with exhaustion and relief. After lunch and what Ian Ostler said was 'the first decent beer for months', they set about the task of dismantling the aircraft and changing the registrations. Exhausted, they fell into bed at midnight and were up again at 0530 the next morning. They then worked for thirty-six hours straight in the stifling heat, loading the helicopters onto waiting air freighters, which Bill Petrie had finally managed to secure without giving the game away.

Jean Dennel took charge of the transport operation. Suitable pallets for the helicopters in the Boeing 747 Cargo and Super Guppy were not available so, while they were being built, the first two Bells were manhandled aboard via a hydraulic lift. A winch was somehow procured to aid the remainder to be loaded.

The jumbo flew to Luxembourg where Frank Chammings and John French, together with a fleet of trucks, waited to take them back to the UK. To avoid problems at Boulogne – the French were supporting the new regime in Iran – and

Home again.
(Photo Malcolm
Pendrill)

contrary to instructions from Redhill, Jean sent the fleet via Zeebrugge in Belgium. He got into trouble with Alan Bristow for getting back too soon – before the press had turned up. For a while afterwards, the hangar at Redhill resembled a Bell production line while Jean and foreman Jack Church directed their reassembly. All seven helicopters were soon redeployed.

Sandstorm was hailed as a thoroughly successful operation. Over the period, thirteen out of twenty-three helicopters had been salvaged: the seven evacuated on the day were worth around $15 million. The 123 members of staff in place at the start of the revolution were all safely evacuated, including twenty-two on the day.

Repercussions were surprisingly low-key. John Black's fake emergency call led to the Kuwaiti authorities banning BHL for four years. Dubai authorities were concerned about the speed with which the Iranian helicopters had become British, but the company was able to show them the correct paperwork.

The remaining Alouettes and Jet Rangers were put under armed guard, then partially dismantled and stored in a hangar. The Kharg B212 was unserviceable, waiting for a new engine. BHL directors Alan Bristow, George and Chris Fry, Bryan Collins, John Howard, together with John Willis, were invited to present themselves at the office of the revolutionary prosecutor at the notorious Evin prison, 'within three days, to give the necessary details to the office'.

Ironically, several of the IHAC clients in Iran, who had not paid the money they owed, said that if they would only return, they would pay their debts. It was, unfortunately, a little late in the day.

Alan Bristow was both relieved and proud.

*It was an episode that I hope will never need repeating. As long as you're engaged in overseas operations, perhaps working in politically unstable countries, you have to face the question of how you might get your people out. You have to be extremely flexible when trying to plan and co-ordinate at long-distance.*

*When you see the efforts to which they go to, in both making those plans and putting them into action, you realise what a high-calibre bunch of people you have on your side. It was a tremendous team effort.*

CHAPTER ELEVEN

# FIFTEEN MINUTES' NOTICE

A military search and rescue service has been in place around the shores of the UK since the days, during the Second World War, of RAF Coastal Command. Its *raison d'être* has always been that of recovering military aircrew, if they were to ditch at sea. However the vast majority, up to 90%, of its missions are invariably in response to civil emergencies.

The armed forces have never objected to this apparent imbalance as SAR missions offer valuable training opportunities and incalculable public relations benefits. However it's an expensive service and ever-increasing demands on capabilities, combined with cutbacks in manpower, mean all three services have to analyse the cost and benefits of every expenditure. SAR training and PR, while still valuable, now come lower down the list than operational capability and 'front-line first'. Since rescues at sea bear little resemblance to the combat SAR missions behind enemy lines, on which they are more likely to be sent these days, the specific training value is less than in the past.

In fact, defence spending has been under pressure for half a century and SAR bases have always been an easy and visible target. Bristow Helicopters first became formally involved in providing rescue services in June 1971, when a WS55-3 (G-AYTK), flown by chief pilot Tony Bates and Lee Smith, moved into RAF Manston in Kent. A standby aircraft, G-AYNP, arrived soon after. They replaced RAF Whirlwinds and were tasked with providing a service along the Straits of Dover, Europe's busiest shipping lanes.

There was a public outcry and many people were outraged at this perceived abdication of government responsibility for rescuing 'their boys'. Despite reassurances that the aircraft was virtually the same and the crews, which would be permanent rather than on a two-year tour, had cut their teeth doing exactly the same job in the Navy or RAF, vigorous lobbying and media pressure took its toll. Despite flying nearly 700 missions and rescuing over 100 people, within three years an RAF Wessex was brought back in. It would be another nine years before the experiment would be repeated.

Whirlwind 3 winch-
training, early 1970s.

Manston SAR unit with the 1972 Wreck Shield. Rear, left to right: Richard Day, Peter Redshaw, Ted
Shepherd, Lee Smith, Tony Bates, Tim Carbis, Richard Drake, Jack Burke. Kneeling: C. Miller, Garry
Williams, Ted Hyde, Pat Ingoldsby, Eddy Jessup.

The first dedicated Bristow SAR helicopter, 1971, over Margate harbour.

In the meantime BHL concentrated its rescue efforts in the oilfields of the North Sea. In the early days it provided an *ad hoc* service in conjunction with its competitor, BEAH. Probably the crews' greatest achievement during this period was in 1974, when they helped to evacuate 150 people from the *Trans Ocean III* and *Trans World 62* rigs after they lost their moorings. Not long after the job was completed, in the obligatory foul weather, *Trans Ocean III* capsized. The pilots, Andy Zgolinski and Malcolm Soper, both received commendations.

Aware of the risks inherent in travelling to and between the early rigs, in 1978 BP sponsored BHL to protect its Forties Field with an offshore-based S61N. During this five-year contract 179 missions were completed. The following year Shell Expro contracted a BHL Bell 212 to provide SAR services within 100 miles of its Brent oilfield. The Bell, with its early auto-hover capability, quickly carved a niche for itself in providing this service. Its rugged airframe and two-bladed configuration meant that it could be hangared offshore in a relatively narrow space. Later a standby B212 was based at Unst, in North Shetland.

On 15 December 1979, the largest helicopter evacuation ever made at sea was undertaken. Fierce storm conditions snapped three of the twelve steel anchor cables holding the Texaco derrick barge *Hermod* adjacent to the Tartan platform, in the northern sector of the North Sea.

As a safety precaution the captain of the barge decided to slip the remaining nine anchors. This manoeuvre initiated the danger of the barge drifting towards rocks on the Scottish coast. To avoid the problems of a full evacuation in worsening conditions at night, the captain called for an emergency evacuation of the whole of the work force – a total of 527 men.

Back at Aberdeen, deputy managing pilot Dave Smith had already decided to suspend flying for the day. Helicopters were being moved into the hangars when the request for assistance arrived. He mustered no fewer than twelve S61Ns and a single 330J Puma, which were crewed by regular line, not SAR trained, personnel.

The helicopters all took off, in conditions that included winds gusting to over 80 knots, frequent snow showers and a 500ft cloud base. Waves were 40ft high and, when they arrived on scene, they could see that the 100,000-ton barge was heaving 20ft vertically, and pitching and rolling way beyond normal helicopter operating conditions.

To try to improve the stability of the barge, cranes on either side of the helideck were cradled. This meant that each helicopter had to manoeuvre rearwards before it could land on the rig. In spite of this, over a seven-hour period, twenty-five round trips of two hours each were made to evacuate the men. The last of the recoveries took place in the dark. Amongst other awards, the crews were later presented with a citation from the Helicopter Association of America.

In November 1981, forty-eight people were rescued from the *Trans World 58* during a severe storm. Such was the strength of the wind, that the two S61Ns didn't have enough fuel to make the return journey to Aberdeen. Instead they flew on to Norway.

Lee SAR.

British Airways Helicopters was first to base a non-dedicated S61N on South Shetland; however, it was always something of a stop-gap measure. It was fitted for but not with a winch and, if needed for a job, it could just as likely be sitting on a platform 150 miles away. Nevertheless, they carried out some difficult rescues with the machine so, soon after, the decision was made to base a SAR machine here full-time.

The process of formalising a service began when, between August and December 1983, the BHL design office and engineers worked to upgrade an S61N to full auto-hover status. Alastair Gordon was the brains between the Louis Newmark LN400-450 auto-hover programme, for both the Bell 212 and the S61N (Chapter 12). They were preparing for a new contract with HM Coastguard (later renamed the Maritime and Coastguard Agency). In December that year a full-time permanent SAR unit was established at Sumburgh Airport, South Shetland. It has been there ever since.

The Sumburgh base would be followed by three more – all competitively bid via the Ministry of Defence (MoD) – on the Isle of Lewis at Stornoway in 1987, at Lee-on-Solent on the South Coast in 1988 and at Portland in Dorset in 1995. BHL was required to fund all the housing requirements for the crews and the Stornoway contract, in particular, required a great deal of research into local conditions. The five-year contracts have continually been renewed.

Specialist equipment developed by Bristow, including a dual electric winch, sea-tray, FLIR and a flat-panel hover stability indicator (HIS), is fitted to the primary S61N at all four bases. The standby aircraft is essentially a standard fleet S61N with some seats removed and a sea-tray and single winch added. It also carries the mountings for a FLIR. The standby does not have auto-hover either, which is a limitation when it comes to over-the-sea rescues at night. The FLIR operator's station is fitted in the cabin, where the winchman looks after it. This is preferred to a cockpit-mounted monitor because the camera tracks in any direction and could distract a pilot at night if it was close to his flight instruments.

The complement at Sumburgh is typical of the other bases. It consists of seven pilots (four captains and three co-pilots), seven winch crew (five dual-role operators and two winchmen), eight engineers, a secretary and a labourer. Year-round they run a twenty-four-hour duty roster, at fifteen minutes standby during the day and forty-five minutes at night (they have to stay within fifteen minutes of the base). Each crew can take up to fifteen hours of training a month but, naturally, the real training value comes from the operations.

These are initiated from Shetland Coastguard station at Lerwick, via a dedicated line. While the rest of the crew run to the aircraft, the captain takes down a brief description of the mission and a position if known. He makes a decision on the fuel load he will need, takes fuel up to that level, starts up and takes off.

The helicopter will fly towards the scene and, if it is a boat or rig, make contact with it from about fifty miles out. It should soon be picked up on the S61N's radar and an intercept made. If it is a drifting vessel or a man in the water, the Coastguard

Lee SAR aircrew, 1988. Left to right: Terry Short, 'Jaffa' Dharamsi and Peter Thompson.

has a software program that is set up with tide predictions and can be programmed with the latest weather. With that, and the knowledge of what the helicopter is looking for, they can predict a start point for the search and advise the best type of pattern to undertake. The information is only good for a short time, but it can be impressively accurate. The pattern can be flown automatically using the HSI.

During a 'creeping line ahead' search the aircraft flies parallel tracks, the system taking account of the wind, with the crew looking out and the winchman operating the chin-mounted forward-looking infrared (FLIR). The FLIR is sensitive to small differences in temperature and, in optimum conditions, the human head can stand out on the monitor like a light bulb. Once the survivor is located the helicopter hovers over him. If this cannot be achieved manually the Newmark LN450 flight path controller is used. Only the winch operator has contact with the survivor and the winch operator has 10% authority over the cyclic. Hover will be held by the LN450 with reference to the Doppler, the winch operator making adjustments if required.

New variable-speed electric hoists give the winch operator the control he needs when, for example, hovering over a pitching boat with his winchman on the end of the wire below, trying to set up a double lift. The primary helicopters now have an identical 600lb-load hoist mounted alongside, that offers true dual redundancy.

It took a while for the Coastguard to start making use of its new assets. During his first two years on the job, Norman Leask – current claimant of the record for the longest-serving civil SAR pilot in the country – recalls being called out on only about thirty-five jobs a year. Since then the figure has risen to around the eighties or nineties – occasionally up to a hundred. Including the training hour allocation, it works out to about 500 flying hours a year per pilot.

*Above:* S61N upgraded FLIR. (Photo Roger D. Smith)

*Left:* First generation FLIR camera.

SAR S61N over the *Piper Alpha* platform, following the disaster in 1988.

The M/V *Lunohods* rescue crew meet HRH Prince Charles. Right to left: Friedie Manson, Kieran Murray, Glen Oldbury and Tony Brewster.

The 'bread and butter stuff' of the unit involves offshore missions, according to Norman.

*We deal with injuries aboard oil rigs or fishing boats – occasionally a sinking – but not much in the way of onshore work such as cliff rescues. In fact, during the 18 years I've been here, I've never actually carried out one of those. If the aeroplane is not available we might get the odd ambulance transfer to Aberdeen, but jobs like that take us off station for several hours.*

*Piper Alpha was a particularly high-profile job but no helicopter actually rescued anyone from the sea: instead we lifted them off boats who had already taken them from the sea.*

For several years in the eighties Shetland was besieged by dozens of Russian and Baltic State fishing factory ships, that would buy whole catches from local fishing boats and process them in bulk. At the height of the activity, ninety-six ships were in Lerwick Sound (their crews essentially doubling the population of the town). Many of these ships were only barely seaworthy and, on several occasions, the Sumburgh SAR was called out to vessels that had broken free from their moorings and drifted helplessly towards the shore. In one particular instance, a ship ran out of fuel. At least three of these were carried onto rocks and had to be evacuated.

One particular crew won several awards for rescuing over sixty Russian seamen – including a record thirty-two survivors in one lift – from the MV *Lunohods*, which

Pip Smith, January 1970.

The *Paraclete* rescue crew with the 1988 Edward & Maisie Lewis Award. Left to right: Andy Hudson, Jeff Todd, Vic Carcass and John Bleadon.

Winch training with a lifeboat.

ran aground below Bressay Point, one November night in a 60-70-knot offshore wind. It broke its back and, to effect the rescue, the helicopter, captained by Tony Brewster, had to hover perilously close to the cliffs, with its tail pointing inland. Sumburgh winchman Friedie Manson, who went down on the wire to organise the recovery, admitted that he had never been so scared in his life.

> *Just after I had sent the first two up in the strop, the bow went under and a wave washed over the top of the bridge where we were standing; sending me and some of the crew sliding along the deck. We found a small gantry behind the bridge that I could hang onto, while continuing to winch the crew to safety.*
>
> *Every fifth or sixth wave crashed right over the top of us and, if it hadn't been for the rails around the gantry, we would have been washed overboard.*

Friedie, who also won the Queen's Gallantry Medal, was supported by pilots Tony Brewster and Glen Oldbury; with winch operator Kieran Murray.

Two out of many SAR achievements by BHL crews in the early days are particularly worthy of mention. In 1968 Capt. Bob Balls, flying a Wessex, transferred forty-five men in three trips from the *Ocean Prince* to another rig, twenty miles away. The *Ocean Prince* sank just after the last group had been lifted off. In November 1969 Capt. Pip Smith evacuated nineteen crew members from the rig *Constellation*, shortly before it capsized while under tow in storm conditions and heavy seas at night. Both pilots were awarded the MBE.

In January 1988 the Stornoway S61N was called out to the fishing vessel *Paraclete*, which was lying about sixty miles off the Butt of Lewis. She had picked up an injured man who had fallen overboard from another boat. The helicopter – crewed by John Bleadon, Andy Hudson, Vic Carcass and Jeff Todd – battled through storm-force winds for an hour to reach the boat.

Attempts to use the 'hi-line' method of recovering the seaman failed and so it was decided to use the conventional winching method. Jeff the winchman was lowered with a stretcher down to the violently pitching deck but as soon as he reached it, he was dragged across it and tossed into a well-deck. Had he not had the presence of mind to disconnect the wire, he would undoubtedly have been killed there and then.

Still connected by the hi-line, the helicopter stood off while Jeff tended to the casualty and strapped him securely into a stretcher. After thirty minutes it moved in

Jeff Todd being presented with the
Prince Philip Helicopter Award
by HM Queen Elizabeth II.

191

'Awright! If you're airsick we won't look!' (Copyright: Tugg, 1982-2003)

for a hi-line transfer – at one point during the operation, the pilots remember seeing the boat and its occupants ahead of them and on the same level. The by-now slack hi-line looped itself around the survivor's neck and Jeff had to quickly cut it before the man was throttled. Eventually both men were recovered and the casualty flown to hospital in Lewis.

John, Andy, Vic and Jeff were subsequently presented with the 1988 Edward & Maisie Lewis Award by HM Queen Elizabeth. Jeff was also awarded the Prince Philip Helicopter Award for that year.

Peter Gray was based at Sumburgh for a short while.

*We were called out a dark December night in 1988, with all the 60s – 60ft cloudbase, 60kts wind in blowing snow, 60ft visibility. A drunken fisherman had fallen overboard and his mates couldn't find him. We launched within the usual two minutes and set up the nav and autopilot for a search pattern.*

*The man was lucky. His head soon appeared as a tiny red blob on the FLIR screen. We punched his position into the GPS and put the aircraft into an auto circuit to arrive overhead in the hover. He was hauled out, covered in blankets and delivered to Sumburgh hospital. All in the dark; nearly all on automatics. He had been in the water for about twenty minutes – another ten would have finished him off.*

On another occasion during the same year, this time at Lee-on-Solent, the duty crew was called out to a yacht that had been seen sailing in a very erratic manner, with no-one visible on board. Two miles behind it drifted its emergency dinghy – also empty. The crew found them about fifteen miles south of the Isle of Wight, drifting south. They lowered the winchman down onto the deck, where he found two Brits – very drunk. They had been on a two-day binge and then decided to sail to France.

The coastguard vessel towed them back into port.

Exploits have never been confined to the S61Ns on permanent SAR standby. In November 1989, two Great Yarmouth-based S76s were called out to Texaco's *Interocean II* jack-up drilling rig, which had lost one of its tow cables in severe and deteriorating weather. Without winches, the plan was to land on the rig's helideck and take crewmembers on board, then shuttle them to the adjacent Shell *Sean Papa* fixed platform.

Although it was already pitching and rolling way beyond normal limits, the first helicopter – flown by Stuart Gregg and Mike Wood – managed to land on and recover the first load of ten passengers. By the time the second S76 – flown by Dale Moon and Roger Williams – arrived on scene, the rig had yawed to the extent that a standard approach was no longer possible. Instead, Dale had to fly up alongside one of the steel legs and fly backwards, without a con, until he could see the helideck. By now the wind was gusting to 75 knots and the seas were later said to be 'massive'.

Dale and Roger made it to the deck and recovered another ten passengers. By now an RAF Sea King and Nimrod reconnaissance aircraft were on the scene. The helicopter attempted a landing on the rig's deck but could not manage it. The weather by now was so bad that the returns rendered the S76 radars useless; instead, they had to be vectored to their target by the Nimrod.

Alan Elphinstone
(left) and Dave Tink.

Both BHL helicopters made a second lift: one taking its passengers to the *Sean Papa* and the other battling 70 knot-headwinds back to Great Yarmouth. Stuart and Mike then returned for a final time but, by now, *Interocean II* had taken on a severe list. As Mike, in the left-hand seat, was manoeuvring close to the rig, it suffered a complete electrical failure. This required a delicate application of power and a rearward touch on the cyclic.

By the time Mike had regained his night vision and switched on the landing lights, the rig's radio operator had switched to emergency power and called for an immediate evacuation of the eleven men still on board. Although the vessel was by now awash at the stern, with the helideck at an increasingly steep angle and moving through fourteen degrees in pitch and roll, in driving rain, Mike managed to land on. He then handed over control to Stuart and supervised the loading of the passengers. Because of the slope of the deck, some of them had to reach the helicopter on their hands and knees, hanging onto the deck netting.

Taking off again produced a transitory overtorque. Stuart and Mike flew back to Great Yarmouth and within twenty minutes the rig had capsized. No one was injured. The four pilots in the S76s shared the 1989 Edward & Maisie Lewis Award, this time presented by the Admiral of the Fleet, Lord Lewin.

In April 2002 Shiner Wright, a winchman with the Stornoway SAR unit, was the first crewmember to be presented with the Billy Deacon SAR Memorial Trophy. The award, which Shiner received from HRH the Duke of Edinburgh, was set up to preserve the memory of Billy Deacon, who was lost at sea during the *Green Lily* rescue in November 1997.

Sponsored by Bristow Helicopters and Breitling UK, the trophy is awarded annually to winch operators/winchmen from the Coastguard, Royal Air Force and Royal Navy for meritorious service during SAR helicopter operations from UK SAR bases.

In November 1997 merchant vessel *Green Lily*, with fifteen crewmembers on board, got into difficulties while dealing with extreme weather conditions, which were estimated as storm force 12 – at the very top of the Beaufort scale. With the vessel floundering, five crewmembers were taken off by the Lerwick lifeboat – its coxswain was awarded the RNLI's Gold Medal, its highest award for courage and seamanship. As the lifeboat was unable to recover the rest of the crew, and with the *Green Lily* very close to the rocky shoreline, the remaining crewmen had to rely on the SAR helicopter for their rescue.

In mountainous seas, Billy was winched down to the vessel's deck. Once on board he placed the remaining crewmembers, two at a time, in the rescue strops and all ten were winched to the safety of the helicopter. As the helicopter was about to recover Billy, who was by now alone on the deck, the boat was dashed on the rocks and he was washed overboard and drowned. In recognition of Billy's outstanding courage and bravery, in the face of the most severe and demanding conditions, he was awarded the George Medal.

Shiner Wright, forty-three, was winchman aboard coastguard helicopter 'Mike Uniform' on the 31 March 2001, when it was called to recover an injured seaman from the fishing vessel *Amadeus,* in 50-knot winds and a violent sea state.

While being lowered to the boat's deck, a severe lurch threw Shiner down into a well deck. Before he had time to disconnect from the winch hook, the vessel fell away once more and Shiner was dragged back upwards, hitting the sides of the well deck and sustaining injuries to his leg, chest and head. As the ship rose upwards again, he was unceremoniously deposited onto the upper deck of the fishing vessel and knocked semi-conscious.

Though disoriented and in extreme pain from a broken foot, bruised ribs and concussion, Shiner managed to disconnect from the winch hook and made his way up to the bridge. Still in severe pain, he administered first aid to the seaman who had an injured shoulder.

G-BDIJ – Lee SAR.

After placing the casualty in a lifting harness, Shiner returned to the winching area and, along with the casualty, was recovered to the helicopter. On return to Stornoway, Shiner was detained in hospital for a short period but returned to work after six weeks of recuperation.

Throughout the rescue, read the citation, his primary concern was for the casualty and he displayed a high degree of determination, dedication and professionalism. As well as holding the Billy Deacon trophy for a year, Shiner was also given a Breitling watch as a personal memento.

Two members of the Stornoway unit completed their 500th SAR missions in the Sikorsky S61N during 2002. Alan Elphinstone has been chief pilot at the unit since its work began in 1987 and winchman Colin Hunter joined only a year later.

Alan marked his 500th SAR mission in the S61N in May. He has flown more than 5,000 hours in Sikorsky aircraft, out of a grand total of over 9,500 flying hours. Colin observed his 500th in September. He has flown more than 3,000 hours in Sikorsky helicopters and has over 6,000 hours in his log-book. Colin's first-ever mission in April 1988 resulted in the birth of a baby in the aircraft.

A government review is currently looking at all aspects of the rescue facilities within and around the UK. It is said to be considering the possibility of having one authority controlling all SAR, mountain rescue and air ambulance assets. It would also establish the preferred relationship between military and civil rescue providers. However the target date for achieving this is said to be 2020.

One aspect of SAR that may be about to change is that of offshore support. While BHL helicopters have been based offshore for many years, their primary mission is not one of rescue and not all have winches. The rescue service has been provided by safety vessels that sail in proximity to the rigs.

However this service is extremely local and doesn't cover the long transits out to, say, the Brae Field. Should an aircraft ditch on its way back to Aberdeen, for example, other helicopters in transit are invariably full of people and unavailable to help. If this should happen, the icy winds and waters of the North Sea mean that time is of the essence.

In 2000 BP identified the potential for improving their rescue facilities and suggested they look at augmenting its safety and support vessels with dedicated SAR helicopters, permanently based offshore to respond to just such an eventuality. It could also get a seriously ill oil-man ashore in half the time it would take, if they had to wait for a helicopter to arrive from Aberdeen.

There was initial uproar from the support vessel crew union, which saw Project Jigsaw as a mere cost-cutting exercise. It also warned that the helicopter would not be able to engage and take off in the worst of North Sea conditions – the most likely conditions for someone to fall overboard, for example.

However a broad consultation process, combined with a commitment to a comprehensive trials programme and reassurances that any service would combine the merits of both air and sea-borne assets, has removed many of these early fears. Trials with a brand new Super Puma Mk2 began early in 2003.

# Awards presented to Bristow Helicopters dedicated SAR units, 1991-2001

| Base | Date | Rescue | Recognition |
|---|---|---|---|
| Manston | 1972 | | Wreck Shield for Meritorious Rescue |
| Stornoway | January 1988 | FV *Paraclete* | Edward & Maisie Lewis Award |
| Stornoway | November 1991 | FV *Burutu* | Chief Coastguard Commendation for Meritorious Service |
| Stornoway | January 1992 | FV *Txori Erreka* | Chief Coastguard Commendation |
| Lee-on-the-Solent | December 1992 | Lulworth Range safety control vessel 8124 | Chief Coastguard's award to duty crew |
| Stornoway | 1992 | – | Silk Cut Nautical Award for Airmanship |
| Sumburgh | January 1993 | MV *Braer* | Aviation Week & Space Technology Laureate |
| Sumburgh | November 1993 | MV *Lunohods* | Queen's Commendation, Rescue Shield, USA Crew of the Year |
| Sumburgh | November 1993 | MV *Brodinskoye Poyle* | Coastguard Rescue Shield |
| Sumburgh | October 1994 | MV *Pionersk* | Edward & Maisie Lewis Award |
| Stornoway | April 1995 | FV *Moraime* | Chief Coastguard Commendation |
| Lee-on-the-Solent | December 1995 | | Chief Coastguard Award |
| Portland | March 1996 | Base jumper trapped on cliff | Department of Transport Rescue Shield, Chief Coastguard Commendations |
| Sumburgh | November 1997 | MV *Green Lily* | Coastguard Rescue Shield, Igor Sikorsky Humanitarian Award, RNLI Vellum, Edward & Maisie Lewis Award, Prince Philip Helicopter Award, Aviation Week & Space Technology 1997 Laureate, Rotor & Wing Rescue Award |
| Stornoway | March 1999 | MV *Multitank Ascania* | Chief Coastguard Commendation |
| Portland | May 2000 | Diver lost in fog | Chief Coastguard Commendation |
| Stornoway | March 2001 | FV *Amadeus* | Billy Deacon Award |
| Stornoway | March 2001 | FV *Hansa* | Sikorsky Winged 'S' Rescue Award, tribute at European Parliament |
| Stornoway | March 2003 | FV *Nuska* | Shephard Press SAR Award |

## CHAPTER TWELVE

# AT THE LEADING EDGE

From the earliest days, when Alan Bristow improvised wooden blade supports for his Hiller in the Antarctic Ocean, to the present, when S61N SAR pilots can accurately monitor hover references at night using flat-panel digital displays, Bristow Helicopters has exploited new technology for its own ends. The goal has always been to make its operations safer and more cost-effective, wherever they take place around the world. Much of the work pioneered by BHL has later been adopted across the arena of public transport helicopter operations.

During the last fifty years many individuals have contributed to this reputation but all would acknowledge the pre-eminent role played by Alastair Gordon – operations director between 1970 and 1989 and deputy managing director-cum-technical services director until his retirement in 1992. He first flew with Alan Bristow on whaling operations in the early fifties.

Throughout his career Gordon, a former Sea Fury pilot and a graduate stress engineer, was the brains and driving force behind many of BHL's technical programmes. These ranged from major innovations like the introduction of auto-hover systems for the S61N and Bell 212 and HUMS (health and usage monitoring system) to the fleet, down to simple improvements like the zigzag rope which encircles the hull of every Bristow S61N. He was the first technical operations manager, with the specific responsibility of identifying emerging technology. As we saw earlier, he was behind the establishment of the BHL pilot training school and involved with the introduction of twin-engined helicopters into company service.

Two of these types, the Wessex 60 and the Bell 212, provided the step-change in performance required by expanding operations at home and abroad. The B212, a rugged and simple twin version of the famous Huey, found an immediate niche in hot and humid conditions and the Wessex, for a while at least, in the more demanding conditions found over the North Sea. Both had attractive power-to-weight ratios and both were certified for flying at night and in poor weather.

Wooden blade supports kept this Air Whaling WS51 secure on deck.

Alastair Gordon.

However the pilots had to be brought up to speed on the subtleties of both twin operations and flying in cloud – while many were familiar with the latter they would spend much of their time trying to avoid it. Alastair Gordon thought that, wherever practical, they should be as comfortable flying in instrument met conditions (IMC) as they were in visual met conditions (VMC). He managed to convince both the CAA and BHL's main competitor at the time, BEA Helicopters, that pilots should be required to reach and maintain an agreed standard in instrument flying and the associated procedures – a forerunner to today's instrument rating which, at the time, was only available to aeroplane pilots. He subsequently devised a company training course which would lead to a pilot qualifying for a 'certificate for flight in instrument conditions'. Nowadays, of course, full CAA/JAA instrument ratings are the norm and the BHL Aberdeen training centre, which now has a deserved world-wide reputation for the quality of its service, prepares pilots for the necessary flight tests.

The other issue which needed resolving, especially where North Sea operations were concerned, was that of icing. The Wessex was prone to this around the engine intake, so Gordon worked with Westland to develop an engine-bleed anti-icing system. To ease the helicopter's operations at the other end of the temperature scale, he also developed a sand filter. This development was overtaken by the arrival of the S61N, so Gordon converted to that type and contributed to the introduction of ice detection systems and procedures on the new machine.

When the S61N entered service it was restricted, in the passenger carrying role, to a maximum all-up-weight of 19,000lb. Military and aerial work operators were able to fly them at up to 20,500lb. Alastair was convinced that operating and maintenance procedures could be devised that would permit safe passenger operations at the higher weight. Trials to demonstrate its single-engined capability in particular were completed, under the supervision of Sikorsky and the CAA.

It was essentially a question of payload. BHL helicopters were routinely configured to take nineteen passengers – the maximum capacity without the need for a cabin attendant – but the permutations provided by this extra payload made the helicopter far more flexible.

In a further attempt to improve payload, Alastair decided to take a leaf out of the airlines' book and introduce to the S61N a fuel dump capability. He saw the benefits as two-fold. In addition to the more obvious one of being able to rapidly reduce weight following the loss of an engine in flight, he saw that payload increases could also be achieved. Lower altitude performance calculations could be made, in the knowledge that the fuel dump would enable minimum safe altitudes to be maintained.

As it turned out, the system never needed to be used in anger following an engine failure after take-off. This was probably just as well – the departure path from the normal southerly runway takes helicopters over the city of Aberdeen, where dumping is prohibited anyway. However, it did allow BHL flights to depart in IFR conditions with enhanced payloads, compared to those of the competition.

When the first Bell 206A Jet Rangers were introduced in 1970, they performed well in the temperate conditions of the UK. In the tropics, however, high turbine temperatures limited the engine output, even though up to 15% more torque was available. Operating on geological survey from unprepared sites in Sumatra, these early Jet Rangers were unable to carry a reasonable payload from jungle clearings, where 200ft towering take-offs over the tree canopy were the order of the day.

Alastair Gordon encouraged the use of a water-methanol injection system that, when squirted into the air intake as the turbine outlet temperature soared, would cool the inlet guide vanes by at least 20 degrees. This would give the pilot enough extra power to climb clear of the jungle canopy. The engineers didn't like the idea – in the first place they had to find the water-meth solution (not always easy in Sumatra) and they were concerned that it might add, in the longer term, to turbine-blade corrosion. Eventually the device was withdrawn from service.

In the early 1970s, Bristow's customer in the Persian Gulf, Abu Dhabi Marine Areas, decided it wanted the additional safety features that were inherent in a twin-engined helicopter. However, the wooden helidecks were not strong enough to take the extra weight of a Wessex 60 – especially with the poor weight distribution from its tricycle undercarriage. Skidded B212s were the answer and, to spread the load even further, Gordon adapted them with snow skis. These proved an incongruous sight over the desert sands.

An engineering training school was set up by John Cotton at Redhill in 1970. At the peak of its activity it employed six instructors and trained over 400 engineers. To some of its overseas customers, a Bristow certificate would be seen as tantamount to a qualification – and often a qualification for promotion.

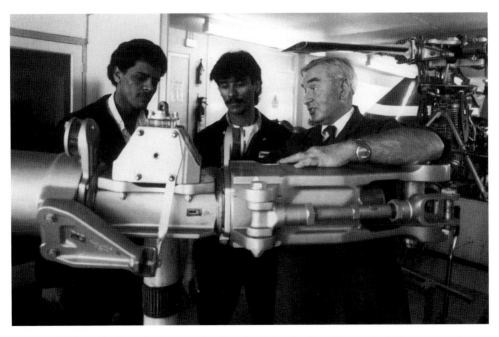

Joe Bowell (right) taught at the Engineering Training School. His motto was 'get it here and roll your sleeves up'. (Photo Malcolm Pendrill)

Left to right: Chief Engineer Ted Everett, together with Gerald Flaws and 'Baz' Leighton, take a break while working on an S58ET.

In the mid–1970s Alastair, intent on reducing BHL's accident rate, set up an in-house flight safety department. It was initially an additional task for flying training superintendent Mike Norris but, as the importance of the work became apparent, it became a full-time job and was entrusted to the very capable hands of Mike Griffin – an ex-Navy maintenance test pilot with an extremely lively and enquiring mind. His skills very much complemented those of Alastair and, together, they constituted a formidable team – the number of accidents attributable to 'pilot error' fell back considerably. Improved maintenance procedures had an even more dramatic effect on hangar-related incidents. They were supported at every turn by Bill Petrie and his engineering team, who were able to put their ideas into action.

By 1975 BHL was essentially an S61N operator in the northern North Sea and a Wessex operator in the Southern sector. However S61 production was about to end and no more Wessex were available. To fill the gap BHL, in a rare and loose alliance with arch-competitor BEA Helicopters, was able to lay its hands on ten piston-engined Sikorsky S58s from the German Air Force. Using Pratt & Whitney PT6-6 Twinpacs, Bristow engineers converted them to S58ETs. BHL retained seven of the machines and BEAH took three. A more comfortable fore-and-aft seating configuration was later designed for both Wessex and S58ET airframes.

To deal with what was now becoming a significant amount of modification work, Alastair Gordon was instrumental in setting up a design office at Redhill. Over the next few years it became so responsive that, if an accident occurred and was found to have been preventable, the company's remedy might be in place before the air accident branch was in a position to publish its recommendations. It was around this time that BHL ordered three new SA330J Pumas, another aircraft designed to fill the gap left by the S61N.

These helicopters, originally designed as military transports, had enormous sliding doors and very small windows, that made the centre-line seating and resulting passenger comfort less than ideal. The fuselage was also quite narrow and, with a low ceiling, made it difficult for passengers to stand up. The new helicopters were initially based at Aberdeen and Sumburgh and later dispatched to Asia and Australia on Shell contracts.

Sikorsky S58ET over Peterhead.

Senior customer support engineer Jeff Kirkup (left) discusses a customer's S76 with Chas Newport.

Bob Salvage, a member of the design office team.

After early problems, the Sikorsky S76 found its spiritual home in the southern North Sea.

The design office was also the cradle for Bristow's new engineering support division which, under Chas Newport, began to sell the company's technical services to military and civil operators around the world. It exported training and engineering expertise and many customers were attracted by the company's reputation for technical excellence. That work kept the Redhill workshops busy with major component overhauls.

When the first SA332L Super Puma arrived, the design office had the factory-fitted seating reconfigured into a more flexible layout. To accompany it, Gordon later devised the first ever helicopter passenger briefing/entertainment system, which enabled safety briefings or music to be piped through to the cabin from a cockpit tape-player. In its early days, passengers had to plug their headsets into a convenient socket – much later a cordless system was introduced.

The Super Puma's much-vaunted rotor-blade and stabiliser de-icing system – a combination of electrical and pneumatic devices – became a real bug-bear and BHL decided to dispense with it. In the UK sector of the North Sea there are very few occasions when helicopters cannot descend towards the sea, where the temperature in the salt-laden atmosphere is almost invariably above freezing point.

The design office developed sponson-mounted flotation devices for the Super Puma.

The emergency rear window on a Super Puma.

In the early days of the Super Puma, BHL decided that it would not adopt a fully-coupled autopilot, instead ordering an uncoupled version. The competition did take the more sophisticated model and that put them at something of an advantage, when pitching the aircraft's MEL (minimum equipment list) during the contract bid process. At the time, the BHL conclusion was that the occasions when a coupled autopilot were required were so few and far between that it was not worth fitting. However, they are now all fully-coupled.

Others contributed more than their fair share to the Super Puma programme. In particular Alastair was supported by French engineer Jean Dennel, who had earlier organised the repatriation of the helicopters from Iran. In turn, he was backed up by technical services manager Chas Newport and avionics manager George Arnold. To take on this new project manager role Jean, as he saw it, was demoted from engineering manager. He complained to Alan Bristow and was told in no uncertain terms 'who better than a bloody Frenchman to give shit to the French?'

It was a pity, say many engineers, that Jean Dennel wasn't available to supervise the introduction of the Sikorsky S76. The early Allison engines were notoriously unreliable and pilots learned to handle the engines, which were essentially Jet Ranger units, with kid gloves. They looked for any twitch of a gauge as a reason to report them as unserviceable.

The straight-through civil design appeared, to start with, to be simply not rugged enough for offshore operations. The wiring was also not well thought of by the electricians and, in the early days, a fractured blade spindle led to a fatal accident off Peterhead. In late 1985, Shell Aircraft removed the S76 from its list of approved equipment. By 1987, new Turbomeca Arriel engines turned the helicopter's fortunes around almost overnight. UK-based S76s now operate from Norwich, which has succeeded North Denes as the BHL base, with others in Australia.

Helicopters with a military heritage, which until relatively recently meant *all* helicopters, are not designed with commercial markets in mind. As a result, in areas such as the size and number of windows, emergency exit routes, the number and stowage of life rafts and the provision of flotation equipment, Alastair Gordon's office had to come up with solutions that could be approved by the ever-vigilant CAA. It also designed the sponson-mounted flotation devices for the Super Puma.

Together with chief test pilot Mike Betts and design manager Allan Brown, Alastair was responsible for the concept of the SAR auto-hover, which is in use today in all UK units. He took a single channel Louis Newmark LN400 system and turned it into a fail-safe duplex operation. Alan Bristow and the board supported him in what was certainly an expensive gamble, but one which has subsequently paid off handsomely. A further notable achievement was the introduction of FLIR (Forward-Looking Infrared) cameras into SAR helicopters, to enable them to search for survivors at night. This was some time before either the police or military took up the idea.

Alastair's enquiring mind did not confine itself to the big issues. After an S61N ditching, when the passengers in the water found difficulties in holding onto the upturned hull, he decided to have a zigzag rope fitted around the entire main fuselage. This way it would work, whichever way up the aircraft floated. He devised a catch to ensure that the cargo door would remain open, if it were pulled all the way back. Without it, if hastily pulled back during an underwater escape, for example, it might swing closed again.

Another incident demonstrated that the predominantly white paint scheme on the BHL S61N made it difficult to spot from the air, were it to ditch and turn over in stormy, wind-lashed seas. Alastair ordered fluorescent chevrons to be painted on the underside of the hull. A remotely deployable life raft was mounted on the inside of the emergency rear opening. If a ditching was imminent the pilot, or someone in the cabin, could jettison the door – which would take the life raft with it. A further modification ensured that the second, forward life raft could be recovered from the aircraft by survivors, even if the aircraft was floating inverted.

Once more ahead of industry and regulators, Alastair proposed that emergency exit windows and doors should be delineated by a form of lighting that would function underwater. The resulting luminescent system became known as EXIS and has saved several lives. Pilots of a Puma J that ditched off Australia, fortunately without passengers, survived because of it and a SAR crewman in the UK was able to escape a ditched S61N by virtue of its escape features. The sudden in-rush of water swept him to the rear of the cabin where, mercifully, he found an air pocket. It was completely dark but he could make out the EXIS outline of the rear opening. The rest of the crew swum around and released it, so he was able to pull himself towards it and safety.

SAR innovations continue to this day. As well as digital hover reference displays, variable-speed dual hoists have recently been fitted to the primary SAR S61Ns at all four BHL/HM Coastguard bases. A fully redundant, variable-speed electric winch system, one mounted outside the other, ensures that if one breaks down the rescue operation can continue unrestricted.

Alastair Gordon's biggest contribution to the broader topic of rotorcraft flight safety, is his work on health and usage monitoring systems – now universally known as HUMS. The principle that offshore helicopters in general would benefit from vibration monitoring was established in 1984, when Gordon contributed to a helicopter airworthiness review panel (HARP) sponsored by the CAA's airworthiness review board. This was tasked with investigating ways of improving helicopter flight safety, a topic which was brought into sharp focus when forty-four people died in a British International Helicopters BV234 Chinook accident on 6 November 1986.

Concerned about the lack of information which became available to them in the wake of this and other accidents, the group recommended the development of a system of sensors, to monitor vibration on vital components including engines, transmissions, gearboxes and rotor systems. It would be able to highlight unusual wear or incipient faults, *before* they got to the stage where they might threaten the safe operation of the helicopter. The readings from each flight would be recorded on tape and removed and analysed at the end, with any unusual 'events' highlighted and subsequently investigated. Over time a comprehensive picture of the 'health' of individual machines would be compiled.

CAD design, HUMS.

Making use of Bristow's own design office, Alastair took it upon himself to build a system. To give him time to concentrate on what evolved into HUMS, in April 1989 he relinquished his position as operations director to Mike Norris, and took on the roles of director technical services and deputy managing director.

BHL had already started to install cockpit voice and flight data recorders, so it was a logical step to extend the parameters and to ensure that the data could be retained after each flight, by downloading from a quick access recorder, rather than overwritten as in the CVR/FDR. When industry as a whole and regulators became involved in this developing technology, the number of parameters and the length of the recording tape became further extended.

HUMS had its detractors, insofar as the benefits of having it were difficult to quantify. Modifying each helicopter meant an expensive operation, both in terms of procuring equipment and in installing it. This also involved a great deal of time – time when it would not be available to earn its keep. If it managed to foresee an imminent accident, that was an obvious benefit but, otherwise, there would be little to show to the bottom line. However, North Sea customers were persuaded of the benefits of the technology and went on to support it financially, while the capital cost was recouped.

Ted Ravenhill (left) and Mike
Cogan in the design office, 1990.

There was also a question of legal liability. If an accident ever happened that HUMS might have predicted, yet failed to, then BHL could find itself involved in some extremely heavy litigation. It was for that reason that the company eventually sold the technology to GEC (now Meggitt) which has since made great headway in introducing HUMS around the world.

Although Bond Helicopters initially bought BHL's package for its own Super Pumas, when Eurocopter eventually came up with its own system, other North Sea operators went for that instead. However BHL maintains that its integrated IHUMS package is the best you can get.

Alastair Gordon saw HUMS introduced to the BHL fleet and retired, at the age of sixty-one, to practise his golf. After he died from prostate cancer in December 1996, the Lee-on-Solent SAR S61N made a fly-past at his funeral. Mike Norris says:

*Alastair was a tremendously popular man. People recognised that he had enormously valuable skills and were prepared, frankly, to go to the ends of the earth for him. He enhanced the company's reputation in the eyes of both our competitors and the regulatory authority.*

*Inertia and lack of helicopter expertise within the Ministry of Aviation, and later the CAA, meant that a solution from Alastair was often well on its way to implementation before its officials had come to grips with the original problem. He came to be regarded as a source of expertise, officials frequently consulted him on the way forward and his presence on the highly influential airworthiness review panel in the 1980s is testament to his standing.*

*As far as Bristow Helicopters is concerned, Alastair Gordon was simply the right man in the right place at the right time.*

Progress and innovation continues at BHL. HUMS has now begat HOMP, a helicopter operations monitoring programme which has completed trials and is now being rolled out across the BHL fleet.

Monitoring pilot performance is nothing new. Known as flight data monitoring, or FDM, British Airways has used it for over thirty years. It uses the information captured by the flight data recorder to highlight departures from normal flying procedures – too much yaw pedal, excursions below decision height for example – so they can be analysed and any lessons passed back.

The key to HOMP's success is the flight data recorder, which has been mandatory since the late eighties, and a CQAR (card quick access recorder) which sits on the centre console. FDR data, collected in a standard crash recorder, remains locked away and is overwritten unless a significant incident is reported. Monitoring data, on the other hand, is routinely extracted on a card slot fitted in the CQAR.

> *When something does go slightly wrong,* [says training captain Nick Norman] *there is rarely time to analyse it on the spot and pilot recollections back at base, especially concerning detail such as gauge readings, can be surprisingly hazy. On occasion, HOMP has shown significant discrepancies between readings that the crew think they generated, and those which are recorded on the CQAR.*

The HOMP system is currently attracting interest from US Army Special Forces and from fractional jet ownership schemes – both of which groups need to know how their aircraft are being flown.

Bell 214ST.

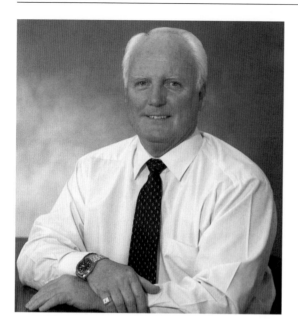

Dennis Russell.

Power-by-the hour is a feature of all major components in BHL Super Pumas and of some, such as the engines in the Bell 214ST and S76, in other types. If engineers uncover a problem – usually through a HUMS trace – instead of investigating the fault they can replace the component and send the suspect one back to the manufacturer. A 'zero-time' and fully updated replacement from the PbH 'pool' is then dispatched.

This comprehensive insurance policy pays dividends for BHL, particularly when a deep-seated problem takes a long time to resolve. For many years, says BHL technical director Dennis Russell, Super Puma gearboxes have had a reputation for making metal. 'It goes right back to the manufacturing process. Any metal chips knocked off internal metal surfaces can generate, via a magnetic plug, a warning in the cockpit. The pilot then has to land somewhere as soon as he safely can.

> It's usually a nuisance rather than a safety issue. Murphy's Law dictates that this will always happen offshore, miles away from engineering support. We then have to send engineers on another helicopter to inspect the plug, drain and replace the oil, carry out hover checks and so on. It has been a long-term problem since Day 1 and, even today, we have to reject more gearboxes than we should.

A process of retro-fitting improved deep-nitrite bearings on the epi-cyclic pinions and faster lubrication pumps, to improve oil flow, is now expected to reduce the incidents of these chips being generated. All this technology is available to BHL within the scheme – other users would have to buy all the components and pay for them to be installed at the next overhaul.

*We save on on-going serviceability checks too.* [says Dennis] *Given the number of hours that we put on our aircraft, and the number of problem gearboxes we've had to deal with, the scheme has been a particularly good investment.*

*The in-house design capability now allows BHL to design its own modifications far faster and cheaper than in the past.*

*The technical services department can sell it to third parties as well. We can design, build, install and approve simple one-off mods, such as fitting a colour radar to a single helicopter, or take on sophisticated projects stretching across entire fleets. When the Defence Helicopter Flying School picked the Bell 412, it decided that the factory-fitted hoists needed to be repositioned, to angle them more towards the cabin door. This involved a major redesign, to create a new mounting that could take all the required loads, without affecting the structural integrity of the main transmission.*

## Dennis is particularly proud of HUMS.

*A huge amount of effort went into it in the early stages but it has certainly paid off. We got the design right and we're constantly trying to update it – changing threshold levels, that sort of thing. It is the operator input that makes the difference. You cannot just bolt it on and go through the motions. We still have daily meetings in Aberdeen, to look through the most recent HUMS data and to see if there's anything that we should be investigating further – any trends that are emerging. It's that sort of attention to detail that gives us a world lead in the technology.*

*HUMS works. It tries to tell you things too. Another operator using our system kept getting indications that there was something wrong with one of his aircraft's tail-rotors. Instead of looking deeper for the cause – investigating why it kept happening – the engineers kept trying to get rid of the effect by balancing it. Sure enough there was an underlying problem: after an in-flight vibration and a precautionary landing, they discovered they had a failed bearing in the tail-rotor hub. HUMS was telling them something was there and they should have predicted that.*

*The new head of an OEM's HUMS project team visited us the other day at Aberdeen. He had been rather thrown in at the deep end and was trying to find out more about the technology. He was astonished to see just how advanced we were in using the system: how we had developed the HOMP tool and how we had sorted out potential 'spy-in-the-cab' objections with the aircrew.*

*He told me afterwards, that he wished he had come to see us guys in the first place.*

## Chapter Thirteen

# SEAT OF THE PANTS

The 1982 Falklands War between Britain and Argentina gave BHL the opportunity to establish its most southerly base since Alan Bristow's whaling days in the Antarctic. The following year three S61Ns (G-BCLD, G-BFMY and G-BBHM) were shipped down to the Falkland Islands in the SS *Ruritania*, initially to operate out of the old airport at RAF Stanley in support of a substantial military garrison. They were off-loaded at the quayside, fitted with their rotor blades and – to the amazement of watching servicemen – flown off to their new home at the airport.

Since arriving there in force after the conflict, the military had realised that helicopters were the only practical and efficient way of moving men and machinery across the often boggy landscape. The only alternatives were Land Rovers or the twin-engined Islander aeroplanes operated by the local air service FIGAS – and they were fully occupied in providing a vital lifeline for isolated farmers.

The eight Bristow pilots and eleven engineers joined a logistics unit with the responsibility for moving troops and loads across the windswept islands. In addition to the civil S61Ns, two military Sea Kings were earmarked for offshore SAR duties and a Chinook for heavy-lift.

The BHL unit moved troops and smaller external loads to isolated military outposts, such as the radar stations at Mount Alice to the south-west, Byron Heights to the north-west and Mount Kent on East Falkland, overlooking Port Stanley. Fuelling points at Fox Bay and Hill Cove needed to be set up and re-supplied and, as tension eased, parties of troops were flown out for R&R visits to local farms. Later an adventurous training centre, where servicemen and women could indulge in hill-climbing and kayaking, was set up at Shag Cove. Finally, the generators at mountain-top radio sites needed diesel, which was flown in 4000lb black plastic sacks known officially as 'air-portable fuel containers' or, more colloquially, as 'bollocks'.

One of the first pilots to make the journey 'down south', Jerry Beecher, decided to go out of curiosity. 'The trip down was an experience – fourteen hours from Ascension Island in an RAF Hercules, air-to-air refuelling, noisy, uncomfortable,

Falkland stalwarts, MY and HM.

S61N Club Class.

Fox Bay refuelling point.

G-BCLD was an early Falklands asset.

either very hot or very cold. All that has changed now, of course, everyone goes the whole way by TriStar. All very civilised.'

The standard duty period was twelve weeks on; then a flight home for six weeks off.

> *Generally speaking we were treated as if we were a unit of RAF Stanley; with all the advantages – such as they were – of being military crews, and none of the disadvantages. When we didn't want to be service people we said we were civilians. Early living conditions, in 'floatel' accommodation barges moored alongside at Port Stanley, were about on a par with an oil rig – apart from the fact that we didn't have our own bathrooms. Instead we used a big communal washplace – but at least it was just for us.*

In the early days, all maintenance was done in the open air and, with the barge accommodation thrown in, life as a whole was fairly rugged. At first, because no winching was involved and load-lifting was carried out using a mirror, the engineers doubled as crewmen. However, that meant they were not available for engineering so in 1990 three specialist crewmen, including the redoubtable Brian Oxley – known, inevitably, as the Ox – were sent to supplement the unit. The Ox, who had served as a specialist loadmaster on the heli-rig project in Indonesia, spent the whole of the rest of the contract with the BHL unit.

Jerry enjoyed his stay in the Falklands for many reasons but top of his list was the fact that the flying took him and the other pilots back to early, more pioneering days.

> *It gave us a rare opportunity to practice seat-of-the-pants flying. When the weather was down – a regular occurrence, whatever the season – you were back to map reading, flying visual, which is certainly not what you do in Aberdeen. It was very satisfying for the aircrew because we were making decisions as we went along. In Aberdeen they give you the book with all the questions and answers and, if it isn't in the book then you don't need to know it. In the Falklands we might come across a challenge while we were flying, and have to come up with the answer pretty quickly. It was good experience for everyone.*

Tony Coleman was probably the longest serving of the BHL Falkland pilots. He spent two years there in the eighties and returned, as managing pilot, for seven more. 'The islands provided a terrific training theatre for our young pilots – lots of low flying with no wire hazards, load-lifting, cross-operating with aircraft carriers and supply ships and ferrying visiting VIPs. Many of our current North Sea captains cut their teeth in the left-hand seat of a Falklands S61N.'

Strong winds posed a constant challenge.

> *It was demanding flying. [says Tony] The potential for damaging turbulence was always there and you couldn't always predict it. I thought I was going to die once when, at 2,000ft near Hill Cove, my speed dropped from 140 to 30 knots – with torque going up and down like the proverbials. And that was in a great big S61N. I was absolutely terrified. We very quickly learned to fly low and keep away from the lee of hills or escarpments.*

LD & MY – and a Tornado on finals. (Photo Paul Boland)

The BHL S-61Ns became known rather predictably as 'Erics', after the darts player Eric Bristow. They played a vital role in the islands, moving troops and external loads to relieve the fully-occupied military garrison. For their part, the military were well satisfied with the service their civilian counterparts delivered. They discovered that Bristow aircraft provided far better availability – between September 1983 and January 1986 the three 'Erics' averaged 115 flying hours a month – and could out-lift the military equivalent helicopters by hundreds of pounds. This was by virtue of the simple fact that they carried less equipment – most of the North Sea navigation equipment had been removed.

Managing pilot during Tony Coleman's first tour (1986-1988) was Mike Bill – who went on to become group admin director – and he was relieved by David Mallock, who hated the 'Eric' sobriquet. On one occasion the pair were flying together and a military air-trafficker casually acknowledged his check-in call with, 'OK Eric, that's copied. QNH is 995 and QFE 998', etc. 'David lost it,' says Tony. 'He railed off against the poor ATCO, insisting that he should be addressed either by his full or abbreviated call sign and that there was no room for falling standards,

HRH Princess Anne visits the Falklands, May 1996.

Refuelling at Fox Bay.

'Steady'.

wherever you might be operating, and so on. Thin end of the wedge, he said. Meanwhile, in the left-hand seat, I was trying to make myself very small indeed. 'When he'd finished his outburst after about what seemed like a full minute, there was a pause and then a tired voice said, 'OK Eric, whatever you say.'

Bristow crews provided a strong element of continuity in the Falklands. Two of its pilots, Simon Wilton and Julie Young – the first ever female Bristow pilot – met while serving in the islands and went back there to get married. Julie went on to become a successful Falkland managing pilot in her own right.

Military units were rotated on a regular basis but, even if their crews went home on leave from time to time, BHL became a constant feature on the islands. The civilians provided an intriguing 'half-way house' for their service counterparts, who showed a great deal of interest in their working methods.

Jerry again: 'Senior RAF officers would come and talk to us, particularly our chief engineer, on a regular basis. They were particularly keen to discover how we could maintain our levels of availability – and at such a competitive rate. There we had to be a bit tactful: the standard answer was that we serviced our aircraft in a different way to those in the armed forces.'

Although the transits themselves weren't particularly long – generally under an hour – the varied payload requirements meant that the S61Ns could rarely carry full fuel.

*In the nine years I spent in the Falklands* [says Tony Coleman] *I could probably count on the fingers of one hand the number of times I flew the exact-same route. Every day brought something different and they used us practically every day. We were so much cheaper than the military – a Sea King would cost double that of an S61N, per flying hour, and a Chinook six times. At the same time we could take nearly double the load of the Sea King – and it had to be a damn big load for it to be worth sending a Chinook.*

Mount Pleasant Airport opened in April 1986 and BHL was one of the first units to move in. The new base offered much-improved accommodation, hangarage and maintenance facilities – as well as a more central point from which to reach the more outlying destinations. In 1987 the establishment was reduced to two S61Ns.

In late 1987, Bob Roffe was called from his desk in the Redhill commercial department for a meeting with the chief inspector of fisheries from the Ministry of Agriculture and Fisheries. Peter Dereham told him that, in order to help the Falkland Islands become financially independent, a reserved fishing zone of 150 mile radius was about to be established. Income would derive from the issuing of fishing licences for both squid and white fish, caught within the zone. The zone itself would be policed by both trawlers and aircraft, and BHL was invited to source a fixed-wing aircraft to add to its helicopter fleet.

Engineer George Fulton prepares a comp wash, Mount Pleasant Airport.

*A Dornier 228 (VP-FBK) soon appeared at Fairoaks Airport, in Surrey, to be modified with the surveillance and recording kit that would enable them to nab boats that failed to pay the exorbitant licence fees the ministry had in mind. 'Zippyquick' training courses were provided to the crews who – to a man – were keen to escape the routine of their regular schedule between Lagos and Port Harcourt. The aircraft was air-freighted to the South Atlantic in a Super Guppy.*

Bob remembers one hiccup in the operation, 'when the Dornier's excellent chief pilot, Harry Hood, was bounced by the MoD for giving tax free NAAFI eggs to the friendly landlord of the Upland Goose Hotel.' This was at a time when all Falkland-native hens appeared to be constipated, and regular supplies had dried up. As far as the army was concerned, this was a scandal of major proportions.

After about two years the island government decided that the Dornier, though fast, was too expensive to run and they were replaced by two slower and poorly-equipped FIGAS Islanders. However the new fishing zone became a great success for the Falkland Islanders and, in a good year, earned the government as much as £28 million.

The Falklands MoD contract came up for renewal in 1997 and, quite unexpectedly, BHL lost it to British International Helicopters. BHL fully expected to be able to carry on – the word was that the respective bids were very close together – and the decision came as a great disappointment.

While BHL was working out the notice period, a third helicopter (G-BFRI) briefly returned to the islands on oil support duties. Between early 1998 and early 1999 it supported a Shell exploration rig drilling in the North Falkland Basin. The operation yielded quite good results but these were not, at the time, considered economically worthwhile. Discussions between the UK, the Falkland Islands and Argentina as to how best to exploit oil and fish stocks to the south-west of the islands continue to this day.

Tony Coleman locked the door on the BHL presence in the Falklands at midnight on 30 June 1998. 'It was the saddest day of my life.' But he believes that the company's contribution demonstrated to the military just how much could be gained by contracting out their support services. It was held up as a prime example of the way forward. 'It was a phenomenal operation. I have to say we did a brilliant job out there, and the army thought we were the dog's whatsits. Much as I love my wife – I'd go back there tomorrow.'

On their way back from the Falklands, the S61Ns headed for Argentina to carry out a joint venture with local operator Helicopteros Marinos, in support of a Mobil offshore drilling programme. They were the first British-registered helicopters to visit the country since the Falklands War. The job lasted about four weeks, after which the two aircraft went their separate ways – to Brazil and the Congo.

The Falklands contract will be up for negotiation in 2005. There may also be an opportunity to take over the SAR commitment from the military garrison. Although the size of that garrison may be reduced, together with the helicopter communications requirement, BHL will doubtless be bidding for the business once again.

The type of aviation support that Coleman and the others provided in the Falklands – flying teams of people over inhospitable landscapes to remote areas – is

UN support in the Balkans.

often exactly what the United Nations requires, whenever the organisation is called upon to support or provide peace-keeping operations around the world. The work itself is usually fairly straightforward – the difficult bit is winning it in the first place. The bidding process is a wide-open book and western operators such as BHL often find themselves out-manoeuvred by others with the availability of far cheaper Mil Mi-8s, for example. However, BHL machines have been working alongside the UN, on international operations, on and off since 1994.

The company's first contract involved sending five B212s to Somalia, to help back-up the peacekeeping operation with passenger and internal freight missions. Four years later, two S61Ns went to Kosovo on a similar mission. One returned after about three months and the second stayed until May 2001, when it was replaced by a B212.

Between July 2000 and August 2002, two S61Ns were sent to the Democratic Republic of Congo, to help military observer teams – known as Milobs – monitor a ceasefire between rebels and government forces. At any one time, four pilots and three engineers would be available to support them.

Falkland veteran Tony Coleman, back home after two years in Nigeria, served throughout this contract. However he doesn't have the same fond memories of this particular phase of his working life.

*I never want to go back there again* [he told Sandie Richardson on his return to Redhill]. *When you leave a place there's usually something you miss. Not the Congo, thanks very much.*

*We couldn't get in to the country to start with and for three months had to stay in Bungui, in the Central African Republic. During that period we flew a grand total of three hours. From there we flew to Freetown, Sierra Leone, for another three months, before finally making it into Kananga, in the DRC, in April 2001.*

*You could see that Kananga had once been a fine town, with all the basic comforts you might expect – mains water and sewage for example – but now nothing worked and the roads were in a dreadful state. Our job was to fly Milobs as far as 150 miles away from Kananga, in order to pinpoint villages and discover whether any rebels were there or not. The maps were next to useless and, at one point, we were reduced to using a 1:2 million-scale road-map, that a Swede in the team had bought in a Stockholm bookshop. Once the front-line had been established we inserted the Milobs, so that they could monitor its withdrawal to the points established by the ceasefire. Finally, we supported the 'away' Milobs with food and supplies.*

*The weather was typical West African, and I was used to that, but living in Kananga was very frustrating because nothing ever worked. In the early days we stayed in the Grand Hotel – something of a misnomer – but moved out after an earthquake brought three naked pilots out onto various balconies. We found that the guest house of a local church had the right number of rooms – there were 12 of us altogether – so we put some effort towards making them comfortable. Redhill sent us a generator so we rigged up some electricity, but there was no air-conditioning and local stand-up fans only lasted a month at a time. As you can imagine, it was extremely hot.*

*Delhi-belly was a problem in the early days but, as time passed, we managed to build up a resistance to it. We had only three cases of malaria during the tour, so that wasn't too bad, but the living conditions and the erratic nature of the work we were doing made it all rather uncomfortable. I was glad to get home.*

## Chapter Fourteen

# EBB AND FLOW

From about 1979 to his retirement in 1985, it became Alan Bristow's habit, as the annual shooting season drew to an end in January, to tour some of his company's international operations. He would book the company's HS125-700 and, together with Chris Fry and on occasion Bryan Collins, set off on a two to three-week programme of visits to bases, either in the Americas or the Middle and Far East. Although the mercurial Bristow could never completely relax, the more usual east-about schedule might include a short holiday in Bali before continuing on to Australia.

These trips were opportunities to visit staff and were generally anticipated – though the long cramped flights in the 'pocket rocket' were considered hard work by Alan's fellow directors. The overseas operations, particularly the Far East one headed by John Willis, had welded themselves into close-knit units that enjoyed a fair amount of autonomy. Nevertheless, it did no harm to keep in touch. Although the 1977 pilots' strike had led to improved communications between management and 'front-line' staff, a popular impression persisted that 'Redhill' was sometimes more than geographically remote from its international operations. These overseas tours were seen as an opportunity to stay in contact. Ever-loyal to his employees, Alan would make a point of learning the names of key staff during the flight sectors, so that he could recognise them at the other end.

They were also an opportunity to talk to customers but, as the years passed, the value of these encounters began to diminish. While in the early days Alan had been chief salesman for his company's services around the world, he would never have claimed any particular diplomatic skills. Back then, business was won on the basis of personal contacts and, to seal the deal, a handshake. By the mid-1980s, however, legions of lawyers and accountants became involved in even the smallest business transaction.

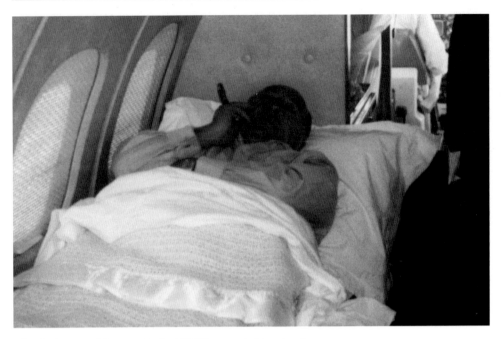

Alan had some of the seats in the HS125 converted to a bunk.

Alan found it frustrating to have to negotiate in this way and his patience often wore thin. During his 1981 tour an argument over billings to GUPCO – the Gulf of Suez partnership between Amoco and the Egyptian General Petroleum Corporation – led to the previously 'evergreen', or rolling contract, being put out to tender and eventually lost to a resident operator. Alan had threatened to suspend operations and this left GUPCO distinctly concerned, that a single expatriate supplier could wield such influence over the day-to-day running of their operations.

Nevertheless, as the 1985 shooting season drew to a close, plans were made for a routine Far East trip in the small jet. It was to feature stops in Cairo, Dubai, Colombo and Singapore, and involved a total flight time of some twenty hours. After visiting John Willis and his team in Singapore, Bristow intended to fly down to Jakarta, both to visit its joint-venture partners since 1968, PT Bristow-Masayu Helicopters, and on a mission, as he saw it, of 'securing our future' in Indonesia.

This visit was planned against the background of a ban on the import of Aerospatiale and Bell helicopters, other than those that were manufactured under licence at the Indonesian IPTN facility at Bandung. The Suharto family also had aspirations to take over local operating companies – including Bristow-Masayu. Earlier meetings with a helpful Foreign & Commonwealth Office had enabled Alan to make contact with Minister for Technology Habibie, who was responsible for the country's oil industry – indeed, most of its manufacturing base. Habibie was known to be acting for the president and had told Bristow that, if he indeed wanted to secure BHL's future, the proportion of local investment in the running of Bristow-

Heli-rigging continued in Indonesia until 1993.

Masayu would have to increase. The alternative was that it would be taken over altogether, by a wholly Indonesian owned and operated company.

In common with most of its long-term overseas contracts, BHL was by now well along the road of recruiting and training Indonesian personnel. As the result of this extensive training programme over the years, it had reduced the expatriate staff involvement to just one of two senior managers. The company was also well aware that the IPTN-built helicopters were significantly more expensive than those of the original manufacturers and took longer to be delivered.

Against this background, and in an endeavour to retain a presence in the country, Alan proposed a cross-investment arrangement whereby Indonesia could invest in the Bristow Helicopter Group. In return, Bristow would invest in Indonesia and, potentially, purchase equipment from IPTN. Alan attempted to persuade his major shareholder, British & Commonwealth Shipping, to support this course of action: however B&C Chairman Lord Cayzer was firmly against the move. He felt that if every country in which the company operated was given this opportunity, then segments of the group could theoretically be sold off to any number of competing interests. There might come a time when they, as original owners, might be in a minority position.

Bryan Collins and Chris Fry, the director with commercial responsibility for the Far East, were asked by Alan to come up with some ideas for solving this problem in time for their visit. He asked them to fax their suggestions over to him at his Cranleigh home, so that he could consider them when shooting had finished for the

Bryan Collins was CEO between 1985 and 1996.
(Photo Morgan Grenfell)

day. On his return Alan telephoned to discuss the proposals: he was not pleased with, as he saw it, a lack of enthusiasm from Bryan and Chris for the cross-investment idea. The following morning, he called Lord Cayzer to recommend his own solution of offering Indonesia the opportunity to take a shareholding in the Bristow Helicopter Group. Sticking to his guns, Lord Cayzer refused to countenance the idea. Alan then offered his resignation, which was accepted. The date was Tuesday 22 January 1985.

Alan Bristow drove into Redhill later that morning to find a hand-delivered letter from Lord Cayzer, confirming acceptance of his resignation and outlining some ideas as to how the transition of power might be achieved. Over lunch with his colleagues that day, Alan suggested that B&C was no longer interested in the future of the business and that its ongoing support was in question. There followed two weeks of legal wrangling and formalities, after which an item appeared in the *Financial Times* announcing his departure by the end of June. By now Alan was in his sixty-third year. Bryan Collins was asked to assume the role of chief executive and Geoff Adkin, finance director of B&C and a non-executive Bristow director, was appointed chairman from Alan's retirement date.

On 28 January Bryan and Chris flew, via scheduled airline, to Jakarta to follow up the discussions. The pair returned on 7 February with a deal which would secure operations in Indonesia for a further eight years. 'There was an agreement to purchase', concludes Chris, 'but it never did happen.'

A difficult period at Redhill ensued. Bryan Collins likened the act of trying to lead the company at the time to 'walking on eggshells'. The main reason for this was that, until his retirement at the end of June and while he was setting up another helicopter business from his estate, B&C had offered Alan the continued use of his Redhill office and secretary. This proved extremely awkward for the other directors. Confirms Bryan: 'it was a delicate situation to have Alan taking lunch in the boardroom where, for the previous twenty years, the most sensitive commercial intelligence had been freely shared between us all.'

Alan was not to be cast off lightly. From his Redhill office and using a new company that he had formed, Bristow Rotorcraft Ltd, he prepared a take-over bid for his first employer, Westland Helicopters. He set up a Swiss company, Baynards Holdings AG, to buy several batches of Westland shares through the market. Alan was beginning to spend some of the £17.5 million that B&C was to pay him, in July 1985, for his remaining 17% share of the Bristow Helicopter Group. But the acquisition plan came to nought.

The very next year, 1986, saw a marked dip in the oil price. Exploration stopped and this, coupled with the effects of some earlier imprudent contract negotiations, saw BHL's profits dip considerably, from around £15 million to £5 million, and large-scale redundancies were announced. At the same time, the new B&C directors were still inclined more towards the financial services sector but the Cayzer family did not agree with this strategy and, for a while, withdrew its private shareholding in B&C.

The shareholding company was renamed British and Commonwealth Holdings and its new chairman, John Gunn, decided to sell the businesses within the group that he deemed not to be core to its new strategy. This group included commercial companies such as BHL and its sister company Airwork, and were bought out by a management team led by Julian Lee, a former partner in Arthur Andersen and an associate of Gunn. This buyout firm, Bricom, completed the takeover in June 1988. Confirming everyone else's worst fears, B&C Holdings used the bulk of the cash from this deal – to acquire Atlantic Computers from John Foulston.

Forecasts were soon back up at the £15 million level but commerce was going through difficult times. Company forecasts had to be strictly adhered to, and Bristow was invariably able to satisfy them. In 1987 BHL bought out British Caledonian Helicopters, including its fleet of Bell 214STs and S61Ns, and in the same year was awarded one of the largest ever contracts for helicopter services. The Marathon Oil (UK) contract involved up to five Super Pumas and required a further extension to the company's Aberdeen terminal.

The Bricom buyout was only in place until July 1990, when the company was bought by Swedish group Gamlestaden – days before Iraq's invasion of Kuwait substantially depressed the oil price. Bryan Collins was convinced the Swedes were with BHL for the long haul even though, under the Civil Aviation Act, they weren't qualified to be in control at all. Instead he knew that they had a dispensation from the then Minister of Transport, Cecil Parkinson. It soon transpired, however, that their intention was to sell off the profitable parts of the Bricom Group – primarily BHL – as soon as practical.

In a bid to forestall this move, in November 1991, the Bristow directors and staff themselves took a 10% stake in their company – in association with venture capitalists Morgan Grenfell (45%) and also Caledonian Investments (45%), which renewed the

Bristow supported the UK Conservative Party during several general elections. During the 1992 campaign, Tim Collins flew Norma and John Major MP.

Cayzer family's association with BHL. They were able to trade very heavily on their own track record to date, and most of the staff were keen to get a slice of the action. It was to prove a wise move and, five years later, the value of their original investments had multiplied six-fold.

Shortly after the buyout, the death of media tycoon Robert Maxwell led to the collapse of British International Helicopters – formerly British Airways Helicopters. BHL was keen to buy the company's assets from the liquidator, with the aim of preventing cut-throat competition between the remaining operators. KLM Helicopters was also trying to get into the UK sector at the time and it succeeded, with the oil companies' help, two years later. However on this occasion BHL withdrew, after the administrator referred its bid to the Office of Fair Trading. BIH was eventually sold to Vancouver-based CHC which, through its later acquisition of Norway's Helikopter Service, also gained control of Bond Helicopters – the third major North Sea player and the descendent of Peterhead-based North Scottish Helicopters.

For the time being under the virtual control of hard-nosed venture capitalists, BHL profitability remained very much under the microscope. After the Maxwell debacle, its employees also needed reassuring about the state of their pension scheme. Some voluntary redundancies, involving pilots, avionics engineers and fitters were requested in 1992.

Bryan Collins says that new MG non-executive directors Robert (now Sir Robert) Smith and Norman Murray were particularly supportive during this period.

Caledonian contributed chairman Peter Buckley and company secretary Jonathan Cartwright completed the team that worked alongside BHL executives. Year on year they increased the volume of business. Despite a temporary blip in 1994, when the oil price became extremely depressed, the company decided to order twenty brand new Mk2 Super Pumas.

By now, BHL's own HUMS suite was mature enough for integration with the Super Puma airframe while on the production line. Eurocopter declined to fit it – having by now developed its own system – as well as the stronger nose-wheel assembly that the operator had requested. Unconvinced that this new helicopter would offer any real commercial improvement over the Mk1 airframes that Alastair Gordon and his team had so extensively modified, BHL eventually cancelled the order.

Venture capitalists usually remain involved in a company only for the short term since, beyond a certain point, the rate-of-return on their investment diminishes. In contrast, Morgan-Grenfell was happy to stay involved until the right buyer came along but, in principle, it was ready to relinquish its shareholding by 1996. There are essentially two ways out of a venture capitalist-assisted buyout – a public offering or a trade purchase – and during 1996 several potential buyers took an interest in taking on a major investment in the company. In December of that year, an approach by long-established US operator Offshore Logistics (OLOG) was taken particularly seriously. There was very little overlap in their respective operations and a tie-up could offer both companies a great deal of commercial and financial influence.

During December 1996, OLOG took over the Morgan-Grenfell shareholding and all of the BHL staff investment. Caledonian increased its own shareholding to 49% and the balance was acquired by Andreas Ugland, whose family owns 51% of BHL's Norwegian partner Norsk Helikopter AS. Norsk was set up in 1993 and operates eight helicopters from five bases on oil support and SAR duties. At about the same time Bryan Collins retired and later moved to the New Forest. He was succeeded by Steve Palframan and, in May 1999, by the present incumbent, former finance director Keith Chanter.

Offshore Logistics acquired the Morgan-Grenfell and BHL management stakes in the business, leaving Caledonian as the only significant external investor. During his interviews for the FD post in the spring of 1997, Keith Chanter was assessed by the senior management from both companies, and he went on the supervise the delicate integration process between two very proud operators.

Keith explains:

> there was very little overlap in our operations – OLOG was big in the Americas and Egypt – and a merger would give us a true global influence. It would also deliver serious economic clout, which would help in future negotiations with our main suppliers, for example. We're now drawing on each others' strengths and best practices and, under the umbrella title of the 'Chrysalis' project, are integrating our IT, finance and engineering supply chain practices. There are real savings to be made from improved management of our suppliers and improved inventory control.
>
> It's a real partnership, because the basic dynamics and priorities of our businesses are exactly the same.

Keith Chanter. CEO 1999 – present.

BHL and OLOG, together, have to deal with the fact that the days of the mammoth offshore project, with its associated numbers of personnel and helicopters, are now over. Through the late 1980s and '90s the advent of sub-sea well development, tied back to existing infrastructures, and automated control systems and production vessels that can be floated from field to field, have led to a reduction in the offshore work force by as much as 30%.

Smart technology requiring less maintenance, and multi-skilling of personnel, has also contributed to this reduction. Helicopter operations have decreased and the market has consolidated, with the oil companies demanding greater efficiency from all aspects of their operations.

Such consolidation led, during the nineties, to the implementation of several redundancy schemes. This inevitably led to some tension within the workforce, yet it came as a complete surprise when one of Keith Chanter's first decisions as CEO, in the summer of 1999, was to ballot them on the subject of union recognition. Out of those who voted, 77% of the staff as a whole and over 95% of the aircrew supported the proposal in principle. BALPA was the clear choice to represent aircrew and, for the engineering staff, MSF was favoured over the AEEU. The company recognised both unions later on that year.

Dave Smith, an ex-Army aviator who had flown WS55-3s and Jet Rangers in Iran, served as Aberdeen general manager from 1995 to August 2000. For the first part of that period he worked under a director, Tony Jones, but took full responsibility in July 1997 after Jones resigned to join British International. After working alongside him for two years, Willie Toner succeeded Dave on his retirement.

Politics played its part in the closure of Unst in 1996. BHL's principal client on the island – Chevron – decided to switch from an S61N operation based there to a Super Puma service from Aberdeen. Shell and the Shetland Island council wanted to increase activity at Sumburgh, with its brand-new facilities, but could not agree on how the costs of keeping the airfield open would be recovered.

BP's Sullom Voe refinery at Scatsta is served by a narrow ex-Second World War aerodrome, with no taxiways. A consortium of five oil companies, led by BP, managed to get a foot-hold in at the facility and helped to lengthen the runway, rebuild the hangar and build a new terminal. Once these new facilities came on stream there was no longer a requirement for Unst, and the continuing high costs of using Sumburgh made Scatsta the centre of the Shetland-based oil industry in 1996.

Meanwhile operations continue around the world. A Bell 212, and for a short time an S61, were sent to Bangladesh to support Cairn Energy's exploration activities offshore. The contract ran from December 1996 to October 1998. In January 2001, Super Puma G-TIGO left Southampton on a freighter bound for Jacksonville, Florida. From there it departed on a five-day ferry flight to Amapa, a city in the state of the same name, to support a six-month-long offshore Brazilian drilling programme for BP.

Drill ship *CR Luigs* was tasked with drilling two holes, thousands of feet below the surface and held on position with GPS-controlled trim engines. The first hole was approximately 200 miles offshore and the second about 175 miles, which gave a round trip sortie time of about three hours. The manifest for the Tiger can include everything from core samples to cauliflowers.

Chris Fry says that an era of partnerships, which now dominate the exploration market, took hold in the mid-1990s.

*This is particularly true of the former Soviet Union, specifically in the area of the Caspian Sea. Kazakhstan is the site of the first joint venture, where we first sent two B212s in late 1998 and which is now known as the North Caspian project. They are based at Atyrau, on the northern coast of the sea, and currently support an AGIP rig situated about 45 miles offshore. We have recently sent out an S76 to carry out ice surveys, and local operator Atyrau Aue Zholy contributes a Tu134 for crew shuttles between Atyrau and Budapest.*

Dallas Brewster is chief pilot on the North Caspian project.

*I helped to set up the JV. It took five months and a lot of effort but it works pretty well now. We carry the usual mix of oil people but, as the programme has a high national profile, we also fly luminaries such as the President of Kazakhstan and special interest groups such as bird-watchers and ecologists.*

*The flying itself is not particularly onerous, he says, but the weather goes from one extreme to the other. Atyrau is built on a marshy coast and endures temperatures ranging between 40°C in the summer and minus 40°C in the winter. Mud prevails during the very short spring and autumn seasons.*

*The weather can be atrocious. The Ural river passes through the centre of Atyrau and freezes on or about 25 November – it's that predictable – and stays that way for three or four months. These temperatures make real difficulties for the engineering staff, led by 'Ringo' Renno, and it is impossible to keep the aircraft themselves much above freezing point. Indeed, the skids get so cold that there is a risk of cracking in the morning. To forestall this we keep two kerosene heaters left on all night, pointing at the aircraft, and fan heaters in the cockpit to try and keep the gyros warm. Wobbly gyros and torque splits are our main problem but, if we run them for a few minutes before taking off, that cures it.*

The marshy environment makes for difficult drilling conditions. The drilling companies have established that lots of oil is there – several North Seas' worth by some accounts – now it is a question of establishing exactly how much and deciding when to harvest it. They also have to maintain the delicate ecological balance and drilling is carried out on a 'no discharge' basis, with waste kept on board the rig until it can be taken ashore by barges.

BHL also established a joint venture with the Government of Turkmenistan in 1999 and provided an S76 in support of a Petronas Carigale programme in the South Caspian Sea. A further JV in the Russian Federation was set up in 2000, when a Tu134 and five Mil Mi-8 helicopters supported a pipeline construction project from Tengis, in Kazakhstan, to Novorossiysk on the Black Sea coast, from where there is access to the Mediterranean. To satisfy the demands of the oil companies, Bristow Helicopters oversaw the technical standards of the operation.

CHAPTER FIFTEEN

# NEXT GENERATION

The Bristow Helicopters' story is almost up to date, but where does the company stand in the year of its Golden Jubilee? After decades of continuous growth there have been periods of great uncertainty; especially during the second half of the '90s. What happened to arrest that decline and what strategy was put in place to help the company face the future with confidence?

Willie Toner – a chartered surveyor with a strong background in the commercial side of the oil business – is director of European operations. When Willie joined Dave Smith in Aberdeen as a manager, at the beginning of 1998, to support him with the more commercial aspects of service company contracting, he knew very little about helicopters. However, crucially, he had firm ideas about what customers wanted from their support contractors and what a contract should deliver to Bristow. By this time, the feeling had taken root in the company that a pilot or engineer, however much he knew about operations, might no longer be best placed to negotiate with the latest generation of oil corporation heavy-hitters.

Within two months of his arrival, in March 1998, BHL won a major contract from British International. The twelve-helicopter agreement with Shell involved operations from Aberdeen, Sumburgh, Norwich and Den Helder and, together with the company's existing client-base, represented as much as 70% of the total UK market. The problem was that the company had just ninety-one days in which to put everything in place.

The announcement initiated a burst of activity. A major recruiting drive for aircrew, engineers and airframes was launched and so much effort was involved that, acknowledges Willie, the company took its eye off the ball. 'Our other customers began to feel uneasy that they were no longer getting the service they deserved.'

In a market dominated by BHL, coupled with oversupply and declining demand, hourly flying rates – which had already been under strain from the low oil price – started to fall even further. To add to the pressure, British International Helicopters, which was owned by Canada's CHC, made a successful bid for Norway's Helikopter

Willie Toner, Director of European Operations.

Service, which happened to own Bond Helicopters. They all joined forces and became CHC Scotia and CHC HS.

> *This was at around the same time as we were trying to renew contracts with Mobil and BP [recalls Willie] and, in late 1998, we found out that BP was looking to move its business. Mobil did the same thing in Spring 1999. Then BP bought Amoco and Arco and those contracts were lost as well. In the space of a few months, from having secured the majority of the market, we were suddenly down to about 40%.*
>
> *The oil price was also down to below $10 a barrel. Activity dried up – we had helicopters parked up with nothing to do – and the world seemed to be falling in on us. Volume was seen to be everything, people were doing anything to win business and, by the beginning of 1999 – only a year after we'd been frantically searching for staff – we were putting together a redundancy programme. We had to let over 100 people go.*
>
> *It was a wake-up call. We had to seriously look at the profitability of the contracts that we still had.*

Shortly afterwards in May 1999, as the BP and Mobil contracts were coming to an end, CEO Steve Palframan left and was replaced by finance director Keith Chanter.

> *It was clear that Aberdeen, as well as the other operations, needed to stand on its own feet so we decided to split the whole company into business units – each responsible for its own accounting, resourcing and service provision. We also focussed hard on the customer service element of our business. Stiff targets were set and the rebuilding began.*

236

Dick Chinn, Business Development
Manager.

The European unit was formed in Aberdeen and led by Willie Toner. 'International', at Redhill, was taken on by Allan Brown and 'Technical Services', also at Redhill, was headed by Ian Ludlow. A corporate management team was set up to support all three cells.

*After analysing all the costs of putting a helicopter in the air'* [says Willie] *'and comparing it with the income from the client, we found we had been running at a significant deficit. So we brought in our accounting function, headed by Ian Dawson, set up a strong commercial team led by Dick Chinn and set off to visit every client we had.*

*We told them, bluntly, that we could not continue with this cut-throat pricing strategy. We were determined to provide a cost-effective service but, like any company, we needed reasonable profits to be able to reinvest in the business.*

*The task of convincing them was extremely difficult but the message got through and, as a result, we managed not only to retain the existing contracts but bring in some new business as well. We've recovered to a market share of around 50%.*

*We run a much leaner operation nowadays but the pressures to cut our operating costs are still strong. The cost of getting a barrel of crude out of the North Sea has always been far higher than that of many other locations and the oil companies are now looking at more automation, remote control and satellite tie-backs, which means less people to move around. Instead of just 'going with the flow', we now try to anticipate changes in the market and, instead of reacting to demands as they happen, we try to be proactive.*

*I believe we're now market leader in terms of quality of service and flight safety – indeed we're a world leader in safety case work and safety management systems. We have plans to reinvest in*

'...Course I've heard of 'em! I make the bloody gravy!!!' (Copyright: Tugg, 1982-2003)

facilities and take on engineering apprentices. We are now working from a firm foundation and the company's reputation for providing high quality and safe services is intact. Client focus and service provision are now key goals.

The oil and gas industry is very cyclical and the new imposed tax increases and current political and economic climates are having an effect on our business. New smaller independent oil companies are emerging and we hope this will reinvigorate demand in the North Sea.

There's still twenty to thirty years' worth of oil left up here and the area remains a very important part of the Bristow portfolio. The outlook remains stable in the short term with, perhaps, a longer term gradual decline on the cards.

Search and rescue represents good business and potential growth. We currently operate four out of twelve SAR bases around the UK and would like this number to increase in the future. We can offer a highly cost-effective alternative to the military operation.

There's no reason, of course, why we shouldn't also export that expertise to other parts of the world. It's all part of the process of marketing our skills.

There is offshore opportunity as well. BP has proposed basing SAR helicopters on platforms, both to supplement the services of its standby vessels and to provide long-range cover for transiting aircraft. This idea has taken shape as the Jigsaw Project and we have an opportunity, using a Super Puma Mk2 on a trial contract, to prove its feasibility. If these trials are successful, they could lead to several dedicated aircraft being based offshore.

Passenger briefing.

Aberdeen passenger terminal.

Commercial Director International,
Allan Brown.

One of the company's earliest overseas operations, stretching back to 1955 and Fison Airwork days, has been in West Africa. Nigeria is still going strong, according to Allan Brown, director of the international business unit.

*We still have the bulk of the business in Nigeria, thanks to the efforts of everyone in our local operating company, which is led by Edu Demola. It's still a growth area: the oil is cheap to get out of the ground and the companies are, only now, starting to look further offshore. Our main base is at Lagos International Airport, where we have a hangar and offices and the renowned BRC (Bristow residential compound). From Lagos we fly oil workers on three Dornier 328 jets down to Port Harcourt and Warri. Until recently we operated a fleet of B212s at those locations but currently fly two S76s and a single B212, while providing crews for six Shell-owned Eurocopter EC155s. Five B212s also fly out of Eket for Mobil.*

*We've replaced many of the expats with Nigerian nationals and each year put three or four pilots through ab initio training in Florida and engineers through AST in Perth. Our Ops Manager, who everybody knows as 'Captain Oni', joined as an engineer in 1984, qualified as a pilot in 1986 and, while working as deputy to general manager Dave Reid, is now studying for an MBA. Senior Licensed Engineer Ike Israel joined the company in March 1975 and has been in Nigeria since 1979. However, there is still a core of expats. Some have settled in the area and one engineer, Chris Tait, has just retired after at least 18 years working there.*

*We also work in Benin, Mauritania and Togo. All three show promise but Mauritania, in particular, has real potential. We've had operations there, on and off, since the sixties but it looks as though the area is about to come good at last.*

A Bell 212 at Warri, Nigeria.

Warri, Nigeria, 1993.

Bristow Australia Super Puma.

Australia is still solid. We have offices and a hangar at Jandakot Airport, near Perth, but our main operations are still for Woodside Petroleum off the north-western shelf. We fly from two Super Pumas and three S76s from Karratha, and two Super Pumas from Darwin. Now and again we fly to Broome, because a lot of exploration is still in the area.

We run a unique operation at Barrow Island. The oil companies there have formed a consortium and we manage an Avro 146 service to bring their new crews from Perth. From there we fly them to the rigs in three S76s, bring out the old crews and fly them back to Perth. This happens six or seven times a week.

We're looking to expand in China. After fifteen years we still fly from Xili heliport. The operation is an hour's ferry ride up the Pearl River, where we have three G-registered Super Pumas subcontracted to COHC. The company has bought three Super Pumas and we have helped train their crews and import the Bristow maintenance model. We have taken a share in the company's GAMEC maintenance company, which supplies facilities to the fast-growing Chinese market for small helicopters. Many of these are Eurocopter machines, some built under licence, and we are sure that bigger helicopters and more services – such as avionics – will follow.

We have an Indian operation, with a B212 and an AS355 working with our partners Deccan at Bangalore, and an office in Singapore from where Catherine Teo works extremely hard on our behalf. She acts as an intermediary with the Singapore government – we have an air force maintenance contract to look after their Super Pumas in Oakey, Queensland.

Bristow/COHC Tiger underslinging flare-stack.

*There's still plenty of overseas opportunity for our services. Over the last 50 years we've flown all over the world, in every extreme of climate and terrain, and have enormous expertise that we can bring to bear – either with our own operations or as part of a joint venture. It is an exciting future.*

The third business unit was formally launched in January 2002, when the internal technical services division was reborn as Bristow Technical Services Ltd. The company's managing director is Ian Ludlow, assisted by financial director Katharine Elliott, production manager Paul Kear and engineering manager Bob Taylor.

*When you've been used to a way of doing business for so long* [says Ian] *'it takes a lot of time and effort to transform an internal organisation into a truly outward-facing business. You have to change everyone's perception – both internally and externally.*

*To compete effectively you must understand your customer needs and then work hard to match them to the services you provide. That is why we have become a lot more visible at trade shows such as Farnborough. I know we have a strong maintenance and overhaul pedigree but we can also deliver world-class design and manufacturing capabilities. These have grown from Alastair Gordon's ideas in the '70s.*

*It is early days yet but we have made some progress. Important external work to date has included a project for the Bundesgrenzschutz – the German border guard service. We have integrated new communications suites and NVG (night vision goggle) capabilities into four of their Bell B212s. We have also carried out some sophisticated systems integration work on FBH B412s, including the fitting of four-axis autopilots, NVG capability and new winches.*

*We supply engineers and/or aircrew to the police air wings of several Gulf states. If one of them has a training requirement, we can arrange the classroom work at centres such as Oxford and carry out any on-the-job training here at Redhill.*

Barrow Island – a unique operation.

MD Technical Services, Ian Ludlow.

The accident rate at Bristow used to be around four to five times the fixed-wing average and it only started to improve once the decision was made, by Alastair Gordon, to enable the offshore fleet to operate under Instrument Flight Rules. The advent of HUMS reduced that again and now the helicopter operations monitoring programme (HOMP) is making a further contribution.

A flight safety management centre at Aberdeen, now headed by Derek Whatling and supported by Tim Glasspool and Nikki McGregor, runs a world-respected safety and risk management service across the Bristow group. Working to Alastair's original specifications, Mike Griffin's contribution in the field has been recognised by the UK's national flight safety organisation, which now regards him as one of the 'founding fathers' of modern safety management and offers an annual award in his name.

Now with what most would agree is a mature fleet of helicopters, BHL is looking at new types. Keith Chanter sees next-generation types such as the Agusta Bell AB139, Sikorsky S92 and Eurocopter EC225 as potential replacements for the S61N and Bristow Tiger fleet. It is a difficult market, however, and oil companies are always looking to reduce their costs and maximise the return on their investment.

Keith believes that BHL customers will be prepared to invest in new helicopters, if it can be shown that they offer new levels of safety.

*The subject covers a host of features, [he says] ranging from new standards in HUMS or anti-icing, through safer harnesses and stroking seats to damage-tolerant design criteria. We have to look at new technology but obviously we need something that meets our requirements.*

Between 1995 and 1997, Technical Services brought these six Pumas of the Ejercito de Chile – Brigada d'Aviación (Chilean Air Force) back into service after fifteen years in storage. (Photo Stuart Wakefield)

*The new generation of rotorcraft has the performance to give us the safety margins that we need. In the final analysis, though, it's the customer that chooses the helicopter. One issue at the forefront of everybody's mind is crashworthiness, which covers a whole range of factors. We're working with manufacturers on a number of projects to define the sort of equipment levels that our customers will be prepared to pay for.*

*The European offshore marketplace is relatively mature but some analysts predict an annual decline of as much as eleven percent. If you believed that, then we would only have another ten years before everything dried up. I smile whenever I hear that – they were saying the same thing ten years ago – and I don't believe the decline will be anything like that severe. However, in our future planning we must recognise the likelihood of a degree of slowdown, and make sure our resources are scaled accordingly.*

*Elsewhere in the world, though. we see a completely different picture. There is a shift in emphasis in Nigeria towards a deepwater environment and a growing marketplace in the former Soviet Union. Many western companies, including Bristow, are teaming up with either local government or local oil companies to figure out new ways of doing business in these regions.*

*Sometimes, as in Kazakhstan, we can use our own aircraft. Under different circumstances the operator may only be able to use Russian-built machines; in which case we want to be able to sell our experience to help our partners provide that service to 'western' standards. On the Caspian pipeline contract, for example, we don't use BHL helicopters at all. Instead our people*

Bristow maintenance – 'second to none'.

'A vast amount
of technical
ability'.

are in management roles, making sure the customer gets the right mix of fixed and rotary-wing support wherever and whenever he needs it.

Nevertheless, [Keith continues] if we were to confine our efforts to supporting the oil industry, there's no denying that the result would be fairly shallow growth. So we're looking beyond oil. One decision we've made is to further improve our own engineering capabilities; with a view to then selling a cost-effective service to third parties, while providing a lower cost maintenance option to out own helicopter fleet.

The only way we can expand is through marketing our own skills. Bristow's Aberdeen engineering and maintenance department, led by Sandy Ogilvie, produces a technical product second to none. The more we can do for ourselves the better off we'll be – and the better placed we'll be towards selling that expertise to third parties. There's strong competition out there but we think our operational expertise gives us an edge.

We are also aiming to further expand our support to the UK Ministry of Defence. Our strategy was moulded by the 1994 defence cost study, which set off a chain of events and led us,

Expanding MoD support.

*a year later, to bid for the Defence Helicopter Flying School contract as part of the FBH consortium. The military's new Joint Helicopter Command is bringing more units together in a single organisation and, with that, comes opportunities for us to offer our engineering skills to maintain, and even operate, many of the aircraft. The DHFS model has been a great success so we're well placed to expand it elsewhere.*

*We have a tremendous experience in operating aircraft and a vast amount of technical ability. If you put the two together and then sell it as a package, you have an almost unique selling point. The original manufacturer can say he built the equipment but nothing can replace years of experience in flying, fixing and flying it again.*

The glory days of the North Sea are long-since past. Exploration continues to the west of Shetland and in the Faroes but new production technology means fewer passengers for BHL. A morning and evening rush-hour has replaced the all-day activity of the 1970s and '80s, as the North Sea industry was constructed. However current business at Aberdeen is stable – conditions which some of the trailblazers might, looking back, have envied.

*We are going the right way now.* [says long-serving operations supervisor Frank Sangster] *We're operating in the black. It's a different management structure. We've trimmed it tight and we are getting better utilisation from both crews and aircraft. As the utilisation is high, our engineering teams are working flat-out as more frequent visits for scheduled maintenance are required. The customers are realistic about their requirements and the oil price and our operations, for the moment anyway, are stable'.*

*Bristow is a better company to work for than it's ever been. There have been ups and downs over the years but I've enjoyed the ride.*

When John Odlin joined Bristow Helicopters from Fison Airwork in 1960, he asked Alan Green whether he might have missed out on the company's heyday. Mike Norris, when he arrived in 1966, asked Alastair Gordon much the same thing. Keith Chanter repeated the question to Chris Fry in 1997 and Willie Toner asked Dave Smith in 1998.

They all got the same answer. 'Not by a long chalk.'

# APPENDIX

Following a dressing-down by the CAA, after being caught low-flying in London in 1955, Alan Green penned the following heartfelt scripture:

## THE BOOK OF IGOR

### Chapter I

And it came to pass that there dwelt in a far-off land a certain wise man.

And the man's name was Igor, and he dreamed of many things. And in his dreams he saw strange chariots which had the eye of man never before beholden, ascending into the heavens and likewise descending again onto the same spot on the face of the earth.

And when he spake of these things, and told of his dreams to the multitude, they laughed at him and cried, 'who is this man who has come among us and who seeks to destroy the teachings of our fathers, of our forefathers, yea, and even the holy teachings of our prophets, the brethren Orville and Wilbur?'

And they rent their clothes in their wrath, and cried out that he should depart from their midst.

And the man called Igor, despite these things, despaired not, for he was of stout heart. And he took himself and his followers unto a remote place and there did build the strange chariot that he had seen in his dreams.

And on the morning before the Sabbath, he climbed up into the seat of his strange chariot, and rose like an eagle, ascending into the heavens, yea, even without the need of a runway, and likewise descending unto the same spot on the face of the earth.

And the heart of the man called Igor and those of his followers were glad, and there was great rejoicing throughout their camp, and they sang praises unto the Lord for many days.

And the man called Igor became known to all men as Igor the Prophet. And his teachings spread to many lands.

And his disciples were many, numbering in their midst men of great wisdom. Williams called Fitz, Bennett the Doctor, and Raoul of Filton, and others also, those of courage and strength who spread the world of Igor the Prophet unto distant lands.

And the word grew and flourished, and everywhere men heard the teachings of Igor the Prophet, and they gave thanks.

And Igor the Prophet and his disciples built many more of this strange chariot which went about their ways, doing good and bringing succour to the sick, and to all manner of peoples.

And wheresoever the strange chariots were seen, not a hair of any man's head was harmed.

## Chapter II

But there was in a certain land a great temple. And the temple was called the House of Ariel, in the street called Theobald, in the city of smoke. And in this temple were many chambers, wherein dwelt divers scribes and Pharisees who hearkened not to the words of the gospel of Igor the Prophet.

For they were men of idle means, who were likened unto the foolish virgins, inasmuch as they cared naught for the morrow.

And they murmured among themselves, and schemed together how they could bring shame and sorrow upon Igor the Prophet, upon his teachings, and upon his disciples.

And like the jackals of the desert, they abided their time and waited until the hour should come.

And it came to pass that on the fifth day of the Feast of Farnborough, a certain young charioteer was journeying from Woolwich unto Croydon.

And as he journeyed in his strange chariot he sang, for his heart was pure and glad, for although but a humble follower of Igor the Prophet, he had helped to spread the word in many places.

And he knew not that the eyes of those same scribes and Pharisees that dwelt in the temples of the wicked were upon him.

For on his return they stood before him and accused him saying, 'thou evil doer, thou hast sinned. For is it not written that man shall not journey below 1,000 cubits, unless it be with the holy parchment from the Most High Pharisee himself, and thou hast done so yea, even below the level of two score and ten.

'Thou shall stand trial before the court of the land and we shall bear witness against thee, and verily thy name shall be damned for evermore.'

And the young charioteer was sore afraid, and sought counsel with the wise men.

And they bade him be of good cheer, and fear not.

And it came to pass that the young charioteer was brought before the court of the land, and the scribes and Pharisees from the House called Ariel stood before him, and accused him again.

And the judge turned to him and said, 'what sayest thou?'

And the young charioteer lifted up his voice and said, 'aye, verily have I sinned against the word, as the word is written. For is not the word according only to the teachings of your prophets, the brethren Orville and Wilbur, against whom no man dare speak?

'But I follow the gospel of Igor the Prophet, who writes that I may journey in peace below 1,000 cubits, and who teaches that it is better for a man to ascend unto heaven up the vertical and twisting path, than for him to journey thence along the broad and legal road as is found by the synagogue and palaces of thy shrine Heathen Row?'

And as he spake there came a great tumult and shouting, and the scribes and Pharisees from the House called Ariel could be heard above it all crying, 'Blasphemer! Sorcerer! Away with him, this wretched sinner, away with him, this wicked man!'

And the young charioteer was cast into the den of lions, and there was rejoicing in the House called Ariel.

And when Igor the Prophet, sitting in his tent in a far-off land, heard of these things he was sorely troubled, and likewise were his disciples also.

And a darkness fell upon the earth, upon the city of smoke, and upon the House called Ariel, so that any man might proceed only with he who was called Item Fox Roger.

And the darkness lasted for many years.

Notes: 'Williams called Fitz' refers to Mr Fitzwilliams, chief helicopter designer at Westland. 'Bennett' is Dr Bennett, chief designer of the Fairey Rotordyne and other Fairey rotorcraft. Raoul is the forename of Mr Hafner, chief designer at the Bristol Aeroplane Co., responsible for the design of the Sycamore and Belvedere helicopters.

Igor, of course, is Igor Sikorsky.

Alan Green.

# INDEX